THE FOOD52 COOKBOOK

Volume 2

THE FOOD52 COOKBOOK

Volume 2 Seasonal Recipes from Our Kitchens to Yours

Amanda Hesser
and Merrill Stubbs
and the Food52 Community

*Photographs by Sarah Shatz, with James Ransom,
Melanie Einzig, and Jennifer Causey*

WILLIAM MORROW
An Imprint of HarperCollins *Publishers*

THE FOOD52 COOKBOOK, VOLUME 2. Copyright © 2012 by Food52 Inc.
All rights reserved. Printed in the United States of America. No part of this
book may be used or reproduced in any manner whatsoever without written permission except in the case of brief quotations embodied in critical
articles and reviews. For information address HarperCollins Publishers,
10 East 53rd Street, New York, NY 10022.

HarperCollins books may be purchased for educational, business, or sales
promotional use. For information please write: Special Markets Department,
HarperCollins Publishers, 10 East 53rd Street, New York, NY 10022.

FIRST EDITION

Designed by Leah Carlson-Stanisic
Cover photograph by James Ransom

Library of Congress Cataloging-in-Publication Data has been applied for.

ISBN 978-0-06-188729-1

12 13 14 15 16 ID5/RRD 10 9 8 7 6 5 4 3 2 1

For Food52ers everywhere—we love you all.

CONTENTS

Introduction

When we launched Food52, we weren't trying to create a community. All we knew was that we wanted to build a business—and that we'd start by crowd-sourcing a cookbook. So we got a book deal, built a website, and after a year of recipe contests and photo shoots and coffee guzzling, we did just that: *The Food52 Cookbook* was published by William Morrow in October 2011.

But what we found during that year was that, with this shared mission, a lively community of devoted home cooks swiftly and organically arose. People were hanging out, sharing ideas, contributing to the book, and shaping the content and tone of the site. They helped each other with cooking questions, gently let newcomers in on the culture of the site, and chatted directly with us. A lot. And it was they who helped us figure out what the business would become.

Without us leading them to it, Food52's members formed what we now call a *constructive community*: one that builds, makes, grows, cooks, and does things together. Potlucks were a natural—more than forty were thrown to celebrate the first cookbook's release, from San Francisco to Nigeria. When a young cook named enbe proposed a holiday gift swap, we didn't expect her to convince more than one hundred people to send their homemade ketchup and rum balls jetting cross-country, but she did, and they did, happily. We introduced the Food52 Hotline as a platform for cooks to help each other out, but it was the community that leapt to action every time a fellow cook needed a last-minute substitute for buttermilk or a fix for a sunken cake.

What you'll see in these pages is the result of fifty-two contests from one year in the life of www.food52.com—from Your Best Recipe with Citrus and Olives to Your Best Dirt-Cheap Dinner—plus twenty-three Wildcard winners that we plucked from the community's archives just because we loved them so much.

You'll see the collective creative efforts of a new breed of community, 100,000 members strong (and counting!)—their recipes, comments, confessions, and advice. We hope you'll find them as inspiring as we do.

Amanda & Merrill

FALL

Roasted Red Pepper Soup with Corn and Cilantro

By Oui, Chef / *Serves 6*

WHO: Oui, Chef is a Massachusetts-based writer. He is a father of five and recently took a two-year professional hiatus, during which he moved to France to study the culinary arts. His blog, www .ouichefnetwork.com, explores how our food choices over time affect not only our own health, but also our local food communities and our planet at large. See his recipe for Herbed Beef Skewers with Horseradish Cream on page 189.

WHAT: A beautifully assembled dinner party star, and a soup you'll want to savor the next day for lunch.

HOW: The tomatoes, peppers, shallots, and garlic are roasted until they're smoky and charred. The corn is toasted in a pan with thyme and then tossed with butter. And cilantro oil is brightened with a splash of sherry vinegar.

WHY WE LOVE IT: If you took all the ingredients in this soup, threw them into a pot, and cooked them together, you'd end up with a pretty delicious result. But Oui, Chef took the soup to a new flavor planet.

Soup

5 large red bell peppers, cut in half, cores, seeds, and ribs removed

4 large heirloom tomatoes, cored and quartered

3½ large shallots, 3 halved, remaining ½ shallot minced

8 large garlic cloves, in their skins

Extra virgin olive oil

Kosher salt and freshly ground black pepper

¼ teaspoon smoked paprika

2½ cups chicken stock or low-sodium broth, plus more if needed

2 small ears sweet corn, husked and kernels cut from the cob

2 teaspoons fresh thyme leaves, minced

1 tablespoon unsalted butter

¼ cup crumbled feta cheese

Cilantro Oil

A small bunch of fresh cilantro

Extra virgin olive oil

Sherry vinegar

Kosher salt and freshly ground black pepper

1.   Heat the oven to 425°F.

2.   Toss the peppers, tomatoes, halved shallots, and garlic cloves into a large bowl. Drizzle with a tablespoon or so of olive oil, season generously with salt and pepper and toss to coat. Place the vegetables in a single layer, skin side up, on a baking sheet with a rim.

3.   Roast the vegetables for 45 to 60 minutes, until everything has started to take on a nice charred appearance. Check the shallots and garlic at 45 minutes—if they are soft, remove them from the pan and reserve; if not, leave them in the pan. When the vegetables are done, remove from the oven and let cool slightly.

4.   Carefully peel the charred skin from the peppers and tomatoes. Squeeze the garlic cloves from their skins. Put the tomatoes, peppers, garlic, and halved shallots in a large saucepan, along with the smoked paprika, and chicken stock. Bring to a boil over high heat, then lower the heat to medium and cook, uncovered, for 15 minutes.

5.   Working in batches, puree the soup in a blender and return to a clean saucepan. Taste and adjust the seasoning. Keep the soup warm over low heat.

6.   To make the cilantro oil: Bring a medium saucepan of salted water to a boil. Toss in the cilantro leaves and blanch for about 30 seconds. Drain the cilantro and put it in a bowl of ice water to stop the cooking. Drain again and pat dry. Finely chop the leaves, then toss them in a small bowl with a few tablespoons of olive oil (enough to make a spoonable cilantro oil). Add a splash of sherry vinegar and salt and pepper to taste. Set aside.

7.   Heat a medium sauté pan over a medium heat. Add a splash of olive oil and the minced shallot and cook until the shallot starts to take on some color, 2 to 3 minutes. Add the corn kernels, some salt and pepper, and the thyme and cook for 2 minutes, then toss in the butter; when it has melted, remove the corn from the heat and transfer to a bowl.

8.   To serve, arrange a small pile of the corn in the center of each of 6 warmed soup bowls, pour the soup around, drizzle with some cilantro oil, and sprinkle with a little of the crumbled feta.

WHAT THE COMMUNITY SAID

CSTORDY: "I served it chilled to rave reviews."

MELISSAV: "I know a dish is a keeper when my husband tells me I need to make it for his parents when they come for a visit. He wasn't more than two bites in when he uttered those very words."

TIPS AND TECHNIQUES

OUI, CHEF: "My first thought was to grate a little ricotta salata over the top, but the feta is a nice stand-in."

ZYNCOOKS: "I skipped a few steps in preparing the cilantro oil and simply simmered a bunch of cilantro in about ½ cup olive oil, then let it sit for a few hours. It was great."

Roasted Radish and Potato Salad with Black Mustard and Cumin Seeds

By gingerroot / *Serves 2 or 3*

WHO: gingerroot is an art educator and mother of two who lives in Honolulu. She focuses on "eating locally, cooking globally." See her Chèvre Devils on page 62 and Late-Night Coffee-Brined Chicken on page 201.

WHAT: Tender caramelized root vegetables swathed in a silky, fragrant dressing of yogurt, scallions, toasted cumin and mustard seeds (gingerroot was inspired by a radish raita recipe).

HOW: The radishes are roasted to soften their bite and make them mellow; they retain a slight bitterness that really complements the sweetness of the roasted potatoes.

WHY WE LOVE IT: Fresh lemon juice lifts the whole salad's brightness. This would make a great potluck dish.

1 large Yukon Gold potato, scrubbed and cut into bite-size pieces	½ teaspoon black mustard seeds
Extra virgin olive oil	½ teaspoon cumin seeds
Coarse sea salt and freshly ground black pepper	2 tablespoons fresh lemon juice
8 to 10 radishes, preferably a variety of sizes and types (I used Easter Egg and French Breakfast radishes), trimmed	½ teaspoon sugar
	2 tablespoons whole milk yogurt
	2 tablespoons thinly sliced scallions

1. Heat the oven to 400°F.

2. In a medium bowl, combine the potatoes with a glug or two of olive oil, a good sprinkling of sea salt, and a few grinds of black pepper, tossing to coat evenly. Spread the potatoes in a single layer on a foil-lined baking sheet and roast for 10 minutes (set the bowl aside).

3. Meanwhile, halve or cut any large radishes into wedges; leave smaller ones whole. Combine the radishes with another glug or two of olive oil and some salt and pepper in the same bowl that you tossed the potatoes in; mix well to coat evenly.

4. Using a wooden spatula or spoon, gently push the potatoes around, being careful to keep the skins as intact as possible. Push the potatoes to one side of the baking sheet and add the radishes to the other side in a single layer. Roast for another 10 to 12 minutes, or until the potatoes and radishes are tender, shaking the pan midway through. Remove the baking sheet from the oven and allow the vegetables to cool completely (this will make it easy to remove them from the pan without sticking—especially the potatoes).

5. Meanwhile, in a small sauté pan, heat 1 teaspoon olive oil over medium heat. When it's hot, add the mustard and cumin seeds and gently mix. Cook for about a minute, stirring, until fragrant, being mindful that the mustard seeds will start to pop. (I use my wooden spoon as a shield to keep them from popping all over the place.) Remove the pan from the heat and set aside.

6. Combine the lemon juice, sugar, and ½ teaspoon salt in a small bowl and stir to dissolve.

7. Halve any small radishes and transfer the roasted radishes and potatoes to a bowl. Add the yogurt, mustard and cumin seeds, and scallions, folding with a spatula to combine. Add the lemon juice mixture by the teaspoonful, tasting as you go. (I used 1½ teaspoons.) Cover with plastic wrap and refrigerate for at least an hour to allow the flavors to develop. Bring the salad to room temperature before serving.

SCHLEGELA: "This was fabulous. I had never thought of roasting radishes. Just delish. I used the same seasoning/spices on roasted beets and it was good, though not as perfect as your combination."

GINGERROOT: "Combining the lemon juice with salt and sugar before adding it to the salad is a secret trick from my grandmother's famous (among my family, at least) potato salad recipe."

NOGAGA: "I just made this, but found myself without black mustard seeds. Substituted yellow, and it was delicious! Many thanks!"

Korean Fried Chicken Wings

By ravenouscouple / *Serves 4 to 6*

WHO: ravenouscouple is a Los Angeles–based couple who love to cook Vietnamese food. They write about it on their blog at www.theravenouscouple.com.

WHAT: A chicken wing recipe inspired by "the popular Korean chicken wing craze from chains such as Kyo-Chan and Bon Chon."

HOW: The wings are coated in Wondra flour and then double-fried to render their fat and crisp the skin.

WHY WE LOVE IT: The wings' delicate shells encase succulent meat, and the spicy ginger soy glaze will have you licking your fingers.

Chicken

2½ pounds chicken wings, tips discarded, wings cut apart at the joints

1 cup Wondra flour

1 teaspoon kosher salt

1 teaspoon freshly ground black pepper

Vegetable oil for deep-frying

Glaze

1 cup thinly sliced peeled fresh ginger

3 tablespoons soy sauce

½ cup packed light brown sugar

¼ cup rice vinegar (or white vinegar)

2 tablespoons honey

1 to 2 tablespoons Korean fermented chile or red pepper flakes

1 to 2 tablespoons sesame seeds, toasted (optional)

1. First, prep the chicken wings: Rinse them with cool water and pat dry with paper towels.

2. In a large bowl, combine the Wondra, salt, and pepper. Dredge the chicken wings in the flour mixture to give them a fine, light coating and set them aside on a platter or baking sheet.

3. Heat about 2 inches of vegetable oil to 350°F in a deep fryer or a large deep saucepan. Fry the chicken wings in batches, being careful not to crowd the pan or let the heat dip too much, for 5 minutes. Let the wings cool on a paper-towel-lined baking sheet. Set the pan of oil aside.

4. To make the glaze: In a small saucepan, combine the ginger, soy sauce, brown sugar, 1 cup water, and vinegar and bring to a boil over medium-high heat. Add the honey and fermented chile and boil to reduce the glaze by half—it should have a thick, maple-syrup-like consistency. Set aside.

5. Heat the oil to 350°F again. Fry the wings in batches until crispy golden brown, 5 to 8 minutes. Drain them on a rack or paper towels. While they're still hot, dip the wings in the glaze, or just brush it all over the wings. If desired, top the wings with a generous shower of sesame seeds before serving.

WHAT THE COMMUNITY SAID

COWANEM: "I made these for the last Super Bowl and I still fantasize about them. I'm hoping the Steelers go all the way, but win or lose, these wings will be the superstar of the next Super Bowl Sunday!"

TIPS AND TECHNIQUES

TASTYFISH: "I have been making these since you posted the recipe. I use panko instead of Wondra. My lord, a better wing there has never been."

Pan Bagnat: Le French Tuna Salad Sandwich

By Waverly / *Serves 2*

WHO: Formerly a lawyer, Waverly is now a mother 24/7, living in Texas. She blogs at www.peaceand loveinthekitchen.com.

WHAT: As Waverly notes, this is "the sandwich version of salad Niçoise," with a glorious riot of colors, flavors, and textures.

HOW: The salad is pressed between the garlic-and-oil-slicked halves of a baguette and left in the fridge overnight, which allows all of the juices to soak into the bread. We chose to include both of the optional ingredients—briny artichoke hearts and crisp green beans—and were glad we did.

WHY WE LOVE IT: Pan bagnat (literally, "bathed bread") is a great solution to the brown-bag-lunch dilemma, and Waverly's version is pitch-perfect.

½ crusty French baguette

6 tablespoons extra virgin olive oil, plus more for
   brushing

1 garlic clove, cut in half

4 to 6 fresh basil leaves

One 6-ounce can tuna, preferably packed in
   olive oil (or use albacore packed in water,
   drained well)

¾ cup Niçoise or Kalamata olives, pitted and
   sliced

½ cup thinly sliced red bell pepper

½ small red onion, finely chopped

¼ cup finely chopped fresh flat-leaf parsley

One 8½-ounce jar or can artichoke hearts,
   drained and chopped (optional)

¼ cup blanched haricots verts (French green
   beans), sliced into thirds (optional)

3 tablespoons fresh lemon juice

Sea salt and freshly ground black pepper

1. Slice the baguette lengthwise, in half. Remove some of the insides of the bottom half to create a trough into which the filling will go. Brush both halves with a little olive oil. Rub each with garlic. Line the bottom half of the baguette with the basil leaves.

2. In a medium bowl, combine the tuna, olives, red pepper, red onion, parsley, and artichoke hearts and green beans, if using. In a measuring cup or small bowl, whisk the lemon juice with

the 6 tablespoons olive oil until combined. Pour the vinaigrette over the tuna mixture and stir gently to combine. Season to taste with salt and pepper.

3. Spoon the tuna mixture into the trough of the baguette and top with the other baguette half. Wrap the sandwich tightly in plastic. Put it on a plate and weigh it down by placing a brick or heavy cast iron skillet on it. Refrigerate overnight.

4. The next day, cut the sandwich in half. Enjoy for lunch at home, or wrap in foil and brown-bag it (use a lunch box that will keep the sandwich chilled). Serve with cubes of feta cheese and a tart Granny Smith apple, if you like.

WHAT THE COMMUNITY SAID

BISTRO_GAL: "I thought the basil was genius and added one more layer of delicious flavor. I was a little concerned that it might become soggy, but the crust stayed crusty while the middle was just a perfect medley of flavors."

FIVEANDSPICE: "Had a chance to try this this weekend, and wowzer! It was wonderful. Such a beautiful combination of flavors and colors—it was like a circus. A delicious circus."

OUI, CHEF: "What a beautiful, beautiful thing. Love the bold flavors and the varied textures you include here. Makes me wish all of my meals were a brown-bag lunch."

TIPS AND TECHNIQUES

WAVERLY: "The bread must have a hard crust, or it will fall apart."

GINGERROOT: "I had a little of the tuna mixture left over and enjoyed it on pasta for dinner—yum!"

Roasted Cauliflower with Gremolata Bread Crumbs

By TheThinChef / *Serves 6*

WHO: TheThinChef is a freelance writer and recipe editor in Orlando, Florida. She blogs at www
.thethinchef.com.

WHAT: Two unlikely bedfellows—roasted cauliflower and gremolata—become best friends,
destined to see a lot more of each other in the kitchen.

HOW: Lemon-and-garlic-scented panko crumbs add snap and complexity to sweet caramelized
cauliflower.

WHY WE LOVE IT: You can easily double or triple this dish for a large party. You can also make it
ahead. In fact, we like it best at room temperature, which has an added benefit: if you wait until the
cauliflower is cool to sprinkle the bread crumbs on top, they'll stay good and crisp!

2 large heads cauliflower

6 tablespoons olive oil

½ teaspoon coarse salt

¼ teaspoon freshly ground black pepper

½ cup panko (Japanese bread crumbs)

Grated zest of 1 lemon

2 garlic cloves, finely minced

2 tablespoons roughly chopped fresh flat-leaf
  parsley

1. Heat the oven to 425°F.

2. Trim the tough stems and cores from the cauliflower and discard. Cut the cauliflower into
   small florets and place in a large bowl. Add ¼ cup of the olive oil, ¼ teaspoon of the salt, and
   the pepper; toss to combine.

3. Spread the cauliflower out on 2 large rimmed baking sheets. Roast until the edges start to
   brown, about 20 minutes, stirring halfway through.

4. Meanwhile, heat the remaining 2 tablespoons olive oil in a large sauté pan over medium-high
   heat. Add the panko and the remaining ¼ teaspoon salt and stir to coat the crumbs with the

oil. Cook, stirring constantly, until the bread crumbs are lightly golden. Add the lemon zest and garlic and toss until the mixture is very fragrant and the crumbs are a deep golden brown, about 2 minutes. Transfer to a medium bowl and add the parsley, stirring to combine. Set aside.

5. Remove the cauliflower from the oven and arrange it on a serving platter. Top with the bread crumbs and serve immediately.

WHAT THE COMMUNITY SAID

SEASONISTA: "I made this for Thanksgiving dinner. Delicious! Stood up to the heavy, decadent meal and stood out for being lighter than the average side."

TIPS AND TECHNIQUES

FLOSSY: "Made it for a party, and was so easy to make earlier in the day and then wait to combine the cauliflower and bread crumbs."

Crispy Salt-and-Pepper French Toast

By aliyaleekong / *Serves 4 to 6*

WHO: aliyaleekong is a classically trained chef who has spent time in the kitchens of Jean Georges, Devi, and Per Se. Based in New York City, she blogs at www.aliyaleekong.com.

WHAT: A savory, peppery treat that aliyaleekong ate for breakfast on Sundays as a child: "The fried bread I grew up eating, called *khara pao*, is the South's answer to French toast, typically served with a kicked-up tomato ketchup."

HOW: Day-old bread is soaked in a batter of eggs, scallions, and cilantro, with a hefty kick of black pepper, fried in a skillet, and served with an easy spicy ketchup.

WHY WE LOVE IT: This toast may just make us turn our backs on sweet French toast forever. It pairs well with eggs and bacon, but (dare we say it?) would also make a mean Monte Cristo.

Spicy Ketchup

½ cup ketchup

Sriracha

French Toast

5 large eggs

3 tablespoons half-and-half

1 teaspoon salt

2 teaspoons freshly ground black pepper

1½ tablespoons finely chopped scallions (optional)

1½ tablespoons finely chopped fresh cilantro (optional)

Vegetable oil

1 to 2 tablespoons unsalted butter

Eight ½-inch-thick slices day-old bread, cut on the diagonal into 2 triangles each

1. To make the ketchup: In a small bowl, stir together the ketchup and enough Sriracha to reach your desired heat tolerance. Set aside.

2. To make the French toast: In a bowl or baking dish, beat together the eggs, half-and-half, salt, pepper, and scallions and cilantro, if using.

3. Heat a large skillet over medium-high heat. Cover the bottom of the skillet with a very thin coating of vegetable oil, then add a tablespoon or two of butter for taste and let it melt. Dip 4 or 5 of the bread triangles into the batter, drain off any excess, and place them straight into the hot pan. Fry for 2 to 3 minutes on each side—you want to develop a golden-brown color, and the texture should be crispier than traditional French toast. Put the cooked toasts on a paper-towel-lined plate or rack to drain while you cook the rest.

4. Serve the toasts warm with the spicy ketchup.

WHAT THE COMMUNITY SAID

MKLUG: "I've never liked French toast because I, too, prefer savory stuff . . . but I tried this and it was perfect!"

THIRSCHFELD: "I had homemade ketchup, so I added Sriracha and now I have a new favorite ketchup too. It was a win-win morning."

TIPS AND TECHNIQUES

ALIYALEEKONG: "I like to use a country or Pullman loaf for this. You want it to stand up to the egg batter and not get mushy, so always go for a day-old loaf."

AVIMOM: "Delish! I subbed thyme for the cilantro and shallots for the scallions. Loved it!"

MRSWHEELBARROW: "Thinking it would be fantastic midafternoon with a fino sherry."

Salted Pumpkin Caramels

By cheese1227 / *Makes 64 caramels*

WHO: cheese1227 is a food writer and lifelong student of the culinary arts who resides in Maine. She writes a blog about her adventures in home cooking at www.remakingchristine.com.

WHAT: Caramels that evoke the essence of fall: The earthiness of pumpkin, softened with cream, permeates each chewy bite, followed by a whisper of spice.

HOW: The pumpkin caramels involve several steps, but cheese1227 makes it easy with the precise candy temperatures in her detailed instructions.

WHY WE LOVE IT: The delicate crunch of fleur de sel offsets the sweetness of the candy, and the toasted pepitas give the caramels a beautifully lacquered, dusty green cap.

⅔ cup unsalted pepitas (hulled pumpkin seeds)

4 tablespoons unsalted butter, cut into chunks, plus more for greasing the pan

1½ cups heavy cream

⅔ cup pumpkin puree (canned or fresh)

1 teaspoon pumpkin pie spice

2 cups sugar

½ cup light corn syrup

⅓ cup good maple syrup

1 teaspoon fresh lemon juice

¾ teaspoon fleur de sel

1. Toast the pepitas in a small dry skillet over medium heat until they start to pop, 3 to 5 minutes. Remove from the heat.

2. Line the bottom and sides of an 8-inch square glass baking pan with parchment. Butter the parchment on the sides of the pan. Spread the toasted pepitas evenly over the bottom of the pan.

3. In a medium saucepan, stir together the cream, pumpkin puree, and pumpkin pie spice and get the mixture quite warm over medium heat; it should start to steam gently but not boil. Set aside.

4. In a large heavy pan with sides at least 4 inches high, combine the sugar, corn syrup, maple syrup, and ¼ cup water. Stir over medium-high heat until the sugar is melted, then let the mixture boil, without stirring, until it reaches 244°F on a candy thermometer (the soft ball point).

5. Very carefully stir in the cream and pumpkin mixture and slowly bring it up to 240°F. This can take a while—up to 30 minutes—but don't leave the kitchen! Watch the mixture carefully, and stir it more frequently once it hits 230°F to keep it from burning on the bottom of the pan. As soon as the mixture reaches 240°F, pull it off the heat and stir in the 4 tablespoons of butter and the lemon juice—stir vigorously so that the butter is melted and fully incorporated.

6. Pour the mixture into the prepared pan. Let it cool on a rack for about 30 minutes, then sprinkle the fleur de sel over the top. Let the caramels set fully (at least 2 hours) before using a hot knife to cut them into 1-inch squares and wrapping them individually in waxed paper.

WHAT THE COMMUNITY SAID

JULIEBOULANGERIE: "Still moaning in delight! I used my own pumpkin puree, made with chunks of pumpkin I roasted and then drained for a couple of hours in a strainer. I learned that lesson after a very runny pumpkin pie a few years ago."

BETTY888: "Made these for Thanksgiving and they were wonderful! The recipe was relatively easy, although I did have to exercise patience, which is unnatural and a bit painful for me! I took care to wash down the sides of the pan with a damp pastry brush, and the caramel came out beautifully."

TIPS AND TECHNIQUES

CHEESE1227: "I have held these up to a week, wrapped individually. If you don't want to wrap them, keep the whole slab covered in the fridge. But if you do that, give it a half hour out of the fridge to make cutting them easier."

MAGPROCTOR: "The recipe did make a pretty substantial pile of individually wrapped candies, so I'd plan on either having a large number of family members over or bringing a bag to the office to win the favor of your bosses."

Wicked Witch Martini

By thecrabbycook / *Serves 2*

WHO: Jessica Harper is a performer and author of many children's books. She blogs at www.thecrab bycook.com. Her book *The Crabby Cookbook: Recipes and Rants* was published in December 2010.
WHAT: A wickedly good dirty martini that will keep the grown-ups entertained through trick-or-treat hour—and beyond.
HOW: This drink shakes up quickly, with more vermouth than you might expect, and goes down smooth and strong, just how we like it.
WHY WE LOVE IT: This is a Halloween tradition for thecrabbycook, whose children are now grown: "I dust off my black hat, put on some scary shoes and a bad attitude, and, bearing a broom as a hostess gift, I go off into the night to my friend Lynn's, where I help her make Wicked Witch Martinis."

6 ounces vodka

1 ounce dry vermouth

1 tablespoon olive juice (from the jar)

1 cup ice, cubed

2 stuffed green olives

2 eyeballs (preferably fake)

1. Decorate 2 martini glasses with spiders and cobwebs and place them in the refrigerator to chill.

2. Combine the vodka, vermouth, olive juice, and ice in a cocktail shaker and shake until well chilled, 20 to 30 seconds. Strain into the chilled glasses, add an olive and an eyeball to each, and serve immediately.

WHAT THE COMMUNITY SAID

GOLDGIRL: "Can't think of any reason not to make this right now, sans eyeball."

TIPS AND TECHNIQUES

A&M: The vodka/gin debate is an age-old one (James Bond was in the vodka camp). If you prefer, make yours with gin!

Moorish Paella

By NWB / *Serves 4*

WHO: NWB lives in New York City.

WHAT: A layered dish that reminds us of jambalaya in its burly spirit.

HOW: This complex paella is built phase by phase as ingredients are layered into the paella pan. NWB blends a spice mixture of caraway, smoked and sweet paprikas, and cumin, then adds it a spoonful at a time so the heat and flavors magnify.

WHY WE LOVE IT: This dish is good on its own, but it's also endlessly versatile. NWB says, "I came up with this recipe after a dinner party left me with a few lamb sausages, lots of spices, and half a can of harissa I did not want to waste."

4 bone-in, skin-on chicken thighs (about 12 ounces total)

Salt

1 teaspoon caraway seeds, ground, or 1 teaspoon ground caraway

1 teaspoon smoked paprika (spicy if you like)

1 teaspoon sweet paprika

½ teaspoon ground cumin

4 small or 2 large links merguez sausage (chorizo is a fine substitute)

1 to 2 tablespoons extra virgin olive oil if needed

1 small onion, chopped

1 garlic clove, minced

½ head cauliflower, cored and cut into florets

½ cup dry wine (I used a rosé)

1 tablespoon harissa

One 8-ounce can tomato puree

2 cups Arborio or other short-grain rice

3 cups chicken stock or low-sodium broth

1. Put the chicken thighs in a plastic bag or bowl, sprinkle with a generous amount of salt, and dry-brine in the fridge for at least 1 hour, preferably all day.

2. Mix the spices together in a small bowl with a pinch of salt. Set aside.

3. When ready to assemble the dish, cut the sausage into ½-inch rounds and brown over medium heat in a large heavy frying pan with high sides. (You can leave the sausage in links to brown,

but I prefer to cut them before cooking.) Remove the browned sausage to a large plate and let cool (slice into rounds if you didn't do this earlier). Leave any fat in the pan, but turn off the heat while you prepare the chicken.

4. Pat the chicken dry using paper towels. Add a tablespoon or so of olive oil if you need more fat in the pan and heat over medium-high heat. Brown the chicken, skin side down, for 3 to 5 minutes, or until rich golden brown. Turn over and brown for 2 more minutes. Remove the chicken to the plate with the sausage.

5. Add a little more olive oil to the pan if needed, then add the onion and cook for 3 minutes, until it starts to soften. Add a dash of salt and a teaspoon of the spice mixture, stirring to combine. Add the garlic and cook for 1 minute. Add the cauliflower and cook for 5 minutes, until it begins to soften.

6. Add another teaspoon of the spice mixture, then add the wine and scrape the bottom of the pan to release any browned bits. Cook for a couple of minutes to reduce the wine a little. Add the sausage and harissa and stir until the harissa is well incorporated. Add the tomato puree, stir, and cook for 5 minutes.

7. Add another teaspoon or so of the spice mixture, then add the rice and stir to distribute it evenly. Add the chicken, skin side up, then add the chicken stock and the rest of the spice mixture and season with several pinches of salt. Bring the paella to a boil, then reduce to a simmer and cook until the rice is tender, 20 to 30 minutes (I find this varies depending on the stovetop). You can cover the pan if it seems to be taking a long time to cook. Once the rice is cooked, let the paella sit off the heat for a few minutes before serving.

WHAT THE COMMUNITY SAID

DANAD: "I finally made this, and I put in some shrimp. They were great with the recipe! I used my paella pan for the first time, and since we have an electric stove, we put it on the gas grill outside. The smoky flavor the paella picked up was great."

TIPS AND TECHNIQUES

TEXAS EX: "I had to use andouille, as I could not get merguez (or chorizo, for that matter). It suited the dish perfectly. Thanks!"

Almond Cake with Orange Flower Water Syrup

By amusebouche / *Makes one 9 x 5-inch loaf*

WHO: amusebouche is a student living in Boston; baking is her first love.

WHAT: A golden brown almond cake, perfumed and moistened by an orange flower water syrup.

HOW: With almond meal to provide a hearty texture and yogurt to keep it moist, this cake is light and sweet.

WHY WE LOVE IT: It pairs nicely with tea and a dollop of crème fraîche or unsweetened whipped cream. A bonus? The cake keeps for days in the fridge.

Cake

2 large eggs

1 cup whole milk yogurt

1 cup sugar

⅓ cup vegetable oil

1 teaspoon vanilla extract

1 cup all-purpose flour

1 cup almond meal

⅛ teaspoon salt

1½ teaspoons baking powder

½ teaspoon baking soda

⅓ cup sliced almonds

Syrup

Juice of 1 orange (about ½ cup)

½ cup sugar

2 teaspoons orange flower water

1. To make the cake: Heat the oven to 350°F. Butter and flour a 9 x 5-inch loaf pan.

2. In a large bowl, whisk together the eggs, yogurt, sugar, oil, and vanilla.

3. In another bowl, whisk together the flour, almond meal, salt, baking powder, and baking soda. Add this mixture gradually to the wet ingredients, folding until just combined.

4. Pour the batter into the prepared pan. Sprinkle the sliced almonds evenly over the top and bake for 40 minutes, or until a sharp knife inserted in the center of the cake comes out clean.

5. While the cake is baking, make the syrup: Combine the orange juice, sugar, and orange flower water in a small saucepan and heat over medium heat, stirring, until the sugar has dissolved, 5 to 7 minutes. Remove from the heat.

6. When the cake is done, cool in the pan on a rack for 10 minutes, then use a toothpick to poke holes all over the top of the cake and pour the syrup over. The syrup may puddle in the top at first—don't worry, it will sink in. Allow the cake to cool completely before removing from the pan and serving.

WHAT THE COMMUNITY SAID

THIRSCHFELD: "I'll take mine with tea, a good French vanilla tea, looking out a window in the heart of Paris while it rains, because this looks like it would make you smile at first bite even on a cloudy day."

TIPS AND TECHNIQUES

DANAD: "I made this last night as written except that I added a cup of cranberries. The almond flavor is amazing, and the cake stands quite well on its own. The syrup and almonds make it more of a dessert, but munching on that last bit of cake this morning with my coffee was just as nice."

MONKEYMOM: "This cake is amazing! Moist and light and so easy to make. I added 2½ teaspoons of almond extract and skipped the syrup altogether. So good."

FRANCA: "Not only can I say that this cake is delicous, but it's foolproof too. I forgot to add the oil! It was still ridiculously moist, not to mention tasty. Did I mention I forgot the sliced almonds on top as well? I don't know where my head was—probably talking to one of my kids as I was trying to follow the recipe!"

Caramelized Butternut Squash Wedges with Sage Hazelnut Pesto

By melissav / *Serves 4*

WHO: melissav is a lawyer in Ft. Lauderdale, Florida.

WHAT: Roasted squash wedges with a hint of cayenne for a subtle kick, a pesto that's garlicky without being overpowering, toasted hazelnuts for richness and depth, and ricotta salata for fresh salinity.

HOW: Baked in a 500°F oven, the squash develops gorgeous bronzed edges with an almost candied interior. The pesto comes together easily in the food processor.

WHY WE LOVE IT: Remember that potato chip commercial that said, "Betcha can't eat just one?" Well, that's kind of how we felt eating these squash wedges right out of the bowl. With our fingers.

Squash

2 butternut squash (about 3½ pounds total)

2 tablespoons olive oil

1 teaspoon sugar

1 teaspoon salt

¼ to ½ teaspoon cayenne pepper, or to taste

Pesto

4 to 5 tablespoons olive oil

¼ cup chopped fresh sage

1 garlic clove, smashed

⅓ cup hazelnuts, toasted

6 tablespoons crumbled ricotta salata

Salt

1. To make the squash: Put a rack in the lowest slot in the oven and heat the oven to 500°F. Line a baking sheet with parchment paper.

2. Cut each squash lengthwise in half and scoop out the seeds. Then peel the halves. Cut each squash half crosswise in half, right where the slender part curves out to the bulge. Cut the squash into 1-inch wedges and put the wedges in a large bowl.

3. Toss the squash with the olive oil, sugar, salt, and cayenne. Arrange the wedges in a single layer, cut side down, on the baking sheet.

4. Roast for 10 to 15 minutes, until caramelized. Remove from the oven and flip over. Roast for another 10 to 15 minutes, until caramelized on the second side and cooked through. (The pieces at the edges of the baking sheet will caramelize first, so you'll want to move them around while they roast.)

5. Meanwhile, make the pesto: Warm 3 tablespoons of the olive oil, the sage, and garlic in a small saucepan over very low heat just until the oil bubbles. Pour into a small bowl; reserve the garlic clove.

6. Put the hazelnuts in a food processor with the garlic clove and process until finely chopped. (Alternatively, you can chop them by hand or use a mortar and pestle.) Add them to the bowl with the oil and sage. Add the ricotta salata to the bowl, along with 1 to 2 tablespoons more olive oil, and stir until combined. Salt to taste. This is not a traditional pesto—more nutty than herby, and not so much oil.

7. Once the squash is roasted, put it in a large bowl and toss with pesto to taste. Dig in.

WHAT THE COMMUNITY SAID

MPRIZE: "Without any hyperbole, I must say that this is one of the most delicious things I have ever eaten. Very simple as well, and you really can do the pesto with a mortar and pestle, which makes it nice and chunky."

HEALTHIERKITCHEN: "I made this a while back and loved it, and just made it again this past weekend for a dinner party. . . . The flavors really balance each other out. Really delicious!"

TIPS AND TECHNIQUES

MELISSAV: "The idea to make a pesto using sage was inspired by Judy Rodgers' *Zuni Café Cookbook*. The finished dish is great hot or at room temperature."

ABCDELICIOUS: "I ended up substituting fresh roasted chestnuts for the hazelnuts and was over the moon with the results. I plan on using the pesto with homemade butternut squash ravioli as a first course for Thanksgiving."

Welsh Rarebit with Spinach

By cooklynveg / *Serves 4*

WHO: cooklynveg is a freelance television producer who lives in Brooklyn, New York. A Brit and a vegetarian, she blogs at www.cooklynveg.blogspot.com.

WHAT: A British comfort food staple for everyone's in-between-meal arsenal: a cheesy, mustardy open-faced sandwich that would be a satisfying afternoon snack, or even breakfast with the addition of bangers and eggs.

HOW: Spinach (we used fresh) lightens up a spicy mix of cheddar and mustard that tops the broiled toasts.

WHY WE LOVE IT: This recipe made us wonder why Welsh rarebit has never taken off on this side of the pond. With cooklynveg's version, there's no longer any excuse!

2 cups fresh spinach or ½ cup thawed frozen spinach

1 cup grated cheddar cheese (I used Denhay English cheddar)

½ teaspoon Colman's mustard powder or 1 teaspoon milder prepared mustard

½ teaspoon Worcestershire sauce

Freshly ground black pepper

Dash of milk (about a teaspoon)

4 slices good sturdy bread (please, no Wonder Bread!)

1. If you're using fresh spinach, heat it gently in a sauté pan until wilted, then let cool. When it is cool, squeeze out the excess liquid and roughly chop the spinach. If you're using frozen spinach, simply squeeze out the excess liquid.

2. In a medium bowl, mix together the cheddar, mustard powder, Worcestershire sauce, pepper, and milk. Stir in the chopped spinach.

3. Heat the broiler, with an oven rack positioned 5 to 6 inches below the flame. Put the slices of bread on a baking sheet and broil for a minute or two, watching carefully, until lightly browned on top. Remove from the broiler.

4. Top the untoasted sides of the bread with the cheese mixture, so it's evenly distributed over each slice, and place under the broiler for 2 to 3 minutes, until the cheese is melted and golden. Serve immediately.

WHAT THE COMMUNITY SAID

COOKLYNVEG: "Okay, for those put off by the weird name, don't be afraid—it's basically just melted cheese on toast. This is a very traditional British dish which we frequently ate when I was growing up. . . . When I was small, I thought it was called Welsh rabbit, and it turns out I wasn't far wrong—you can read about its history on Wikipedia."

ANTONIAJAMES: "This was a family favorite of ours when I was growing up (in Virginia), where my mother made it in much the same way. . . . Good sharp cheese and Worcestershire are the keys to this castle."

MCS3000: "Wow! perfect Meatless Monday snack, or anytime."

TIPS AND TECHNIQUES

COOKLYNVEG: "I use Colman's English mustard powder which is very strong and flavorful, but other mustards work equally well—especially a good Dijon or hot whole-grain variety."

KIKIMAMA: "This is really good! I quartered the recipe for lunch for one person, and it worked out very well."

Vegetarian Mushroom Thyme Gravy

By sticksnscones / *Serves 6*

WHO: sticksnscones is a knitting retailer and freelance baker who lives in Massachusetts.

WHAT: A mushroom gravy that solves nearly every Thanksgiving dilemma there is.

HOW: Umami-rich dried mushrooms are used to fortify the stock, and sautéed shallots, soy sauce, fresh thyme, and sherry round out the rich but balanced sauce, which we'd like to pretend is actually a soup.

WHY WE LOVE IT: It's vegetarian-friendly, requires no pan drippings (ideal for when you're deep-frying your bird or brining has rendered the drippings too salty), and comes together in no time, yet it hides deceptively deep layers of flavor.

2 cups vegetable stock	3 tablespoons soy sauce
⅓ cup dried mushrooms (shiitake or mixed)	½ cup light cream
3 tablespoons unsalted butter	1 tablespoon sherry
1½ tablespoons minced shallots	1 tablespoon minced fresh thyme
3 tablespoons all-purpose flour	Salt and freshly ground black pepper

1. Bring the vegetable stock to a boil in a small saucepan. Put the mushrooms in a small bowl and pour the boiling stock over them. Let soak for 20 minutes.

2. Lift out the mushrooms and mince or thinly slice them. Pour 1½ cups of the stock into a large measuring cup, leaving any sediment behind.

3. In a medium saucepan, melt the butter over medium heat. Add the shallots and sauté until softened, about 5 minutes. Add the flour, stirring constantly, and cook, stirring, for 2 minutes.

4. Gradually add the reserved vegetable stock, whisking to incorporate. Cook over medium heat, stirring, until the gravy is thickened. Add the reserved mushrooms, soy sauce, cream, sherry, and thyme and cook for a few more minutes, until heated through and thickened to the desired consistency. Season to taste with salt and pepper.

5. Pour over anything on your plate!

WHAT THE COMMUNITY SAID

OUI, CHEF: "I made this fabulous gravy for Thanksgiving, and while I never say never, I'm having a hard time envisioning going back to a last-minute 'pan-dripping' style of gravy anytime soon. This was TERRIFIC! Thanks for the great recipe."

JIFFERB: "I mixed this with my green beans for a homemade green bean casserole topped with fried onions—not only was the dish gone in minutes, at least five people asked for the recipe. So, sooooo good."

TIPS AND TECHNIQUES

A&M: This gravy can easily be prepared ahead of time and reheated. Heads up: One time when we tested it, we accidentally used just 2 tablespoons of flour, but we ended up really liking that too—it was less creamy and voluptuous, more free-flowing, with a concentrated hit of mushroom flavor and color.

STICKSNSCONES: "You can use any type of dried mushroom. I have used just shiitake mushrooms, but mixed dried mushrooms will provide more interesting flavors. To make a vegan version, substitute olive oil for the butter and additional stock for the cream."

NANKAE: "Didn't have shallots or sherry on hand so I substituted super finely minced white onion and white wine (a Chablis—all we had open). If it's this tasty with those substitutions, I can only imagine how good it would be with the shallots and sherry."

TEXAS EX: "I took advantage of one of Alton Brown's tips and put the prepared gravy in a Thermos until dinner was ready. That technique made the recipe that much better."

Butternut Sage Scones

By mrslarkin / *Makes 8 scones*

WHO: mrslarkin sells scones, cookies, and other baked goods at the Pound Ridge Farmer's Market in Pound Ridge, New York, every Sunday April through November and by special-order. She blogs at www.mrslarkins.com.

WHAT: Incredibly moist scones, perfumed with sage and squash, and as sweet as you want them to be, depending on whether or not you opt for the cinnamon drizzle.

HOW: mrslarkin recommends cooking and draining the squash the day before. She says, "These do look very pretty decorated with the sage leaf on top, so don't skip that step."

WHY WE LOVE IT: We've been lucky enough to taste mrslarkin's goods firsthand, so we knew we had to try making these scones ourselves. Lo and behold, they came out just as delicious as the real thing. If you make these for Thanksgiving breakfast, they won't last till lunch.

Scones

1 small butternut squash

2 cups unbleached all-purpose flour
  (I use King Arthur)

6 tablespoons sugar, plus more for sprinkling

1 tablespoon baking powder

½ teaspoon kosher salt

½ teaspoon ground cinnamon

½ teaspoon freshly grated nutmeg

Scant ¼ teaspoon ground cloves

Scant ¼ teaspoon ground ginger

2 teaspoons finely chopped fresh sage, plus 8
  small sage leaves

6 tablespoons cold unsalted butter, cut into
  small cubes

1 large egg

⅓ cup heavy cream, plus more for brushing

Cinnamon Drizzle (optional)

1 cup confectioners' sugar, or as needed

½ teaspoon ground cinnamon, or to taste

1. To make the scones: Pierce the squash all over with a fork or the tip of a knife. Place in a microwave-safe dish and cook on high for about 30 minutes, turning every 10 minutes or so,

until soft and mushy. Cut the squash open down the middle. If it's still hard in the middle, nuke it a little more. Then let it cool slightly.

2. Remove the squash seeds and pulp. Scoop out the soft squash, mash it a bit, and place in a strainer set over a bowl. Let it drain for at least a couple of hours, or overnight. (You'll probably have extra squash, as the recipe uses only ½ cup. Make soup with the rest, or double the scone recipe.)

3. Heat the oven to 425°F.

4. Place the dry ingredients and chopped sage in the bowl of a food processor and pulse to combine. Add the butter and pulse 10 or so times. You want to retain some small pieces of butter; don't blitz the heck out of it. Transfer the flour mixture to a large bowl. If you've got some really large butter lumps, just squish them with the back of a fork.

5. Place ½ cup squash puree in a large measuring cup, add the egg and heavy cream, and mix well. Pour into the flour mixture. With a fork, fold the wet into the dry as you gradually turn the bowl—it's a folding motion you're shooting for, not a stirring motion. When the dough begins to gather together, use a plastic bowl scraper to gently knead it into a ball.

6. Transfer the dough to a floured board. Gently pat it into a 6-inch circle. With the bowl scraper or large chef's knife, cut it into 8 triangles. (I use a pie marker to score the top of the dough circle and use the lines as a guide.) Optional: Place the scones on a waxed-paper-lined baking sheet and freeze until solid; once they are frozen, you can store them in a plastic freezer bag for several weeks before baking. (Do not thaw them first.)

7. Place the scones on a parchment-lined baking sheet, about 1 inch apart. Brush with cream. Brush the front and back of the whole sage leaves with cream and place on top of the scones. Sprinkle the tops of the scones with sugar.

8. Bake the scones for 20 to 25 minutes, turning the pan halfway through. They are done when a wooden skewer inserted in the center comes out clean. Let cool.

9. If making the cinnamon drizzle: Mix the confectioners' sugar and cinnamon in a small bowl. Add 2 tablespoons warm water and stir until smooth. I always do this by sight. If it is too loose, add more sugar, if too thick, add more water. It should be thick like corn syrup. If it's not cinnamony enough, add more cinnamon. Drizzle on the scones once they're cool.

JOANG: "I just made these tonight with a different winter squash. They are absolutely delicious! My husband hates pumpkin pie and pumpkin bread, but he thought they were great. He especially liked the cinnamon glaze."

GINGERROOT: "Made these for breakfast on Thanksgiving morning and they were amazing. My non-squash-eating daughter immediately devoured two in a row before I told her they were butternut squash. All she could do was grin. Thank you so much for a fantastic recipe!!"

CHEZSUZANNE: "OMG, these are without a doubt the best scones I've ever had! Not too sweet, not too much squash, just the right texture. I love them! They just came out of the oven, I wolfed one down, and I may have to leave the house to prevent myself from eating the other seven before dinner."

TIPS AND TECHNIQUES

MRSLARKIN: "When measuring flour, I usually fluff it with a whisk, scoop it up with a spoon, sprinkle it into the measuring cup, and sweep off the top with the flat edge of a knife or spatula. But when I make scones, I always weigh the flour—and bypass all that extra work.

"I highly recommend you get an oven thermometer if you don't have one already. The success of quick breads like this depend upon a really cranking-hot oven, and if your oven fluctuates, like mine does, then you can adjust your oven temp accordingly. Mine always runs cooler, so I crank it up until the thermometer reads the temp I want. Also, if you are baking less than a full batch, double up on your baking sheets, which will help prevent scorched bottoms.

"You can slather the scones with clotted cream and fig jam if you feel like gilding the lily. But these are pretty darn good with just plain ol' butter too. They are great the next day, warmed in the microwave for 15 to 20 seconds. They freeze really well too, and they can be reheated in a 350°F oven until warm. Enjoy!"

Ginger Apple Torte

By drbabs / *Serves 6 to 8*

WHO: drbabs is an optometrist and food lover who lives in Huntington, New York; see her Shrimp Gumbo on page 153.

WHAT: A fusion of gingerbread and apple cake, with layers of spiced batter enveloping tender caramelized apples and a top coating of turbinado sugar melted into a sturdy, glassy crust.

HOW: Make sure you caramelize the apples when sautéing, so they get a little oomph!

WHY WE LOVE IT: For the batter, drbabs riffed on a gingerbread recipe from Laurie Colwin's *Home Cooking*. She noted, "Ginger is thought to aid digestion, so this is perfect after Thanksgiving dinner."

10 tablespoons (1¼ sticks) unsalted butter, at room temperature, plus more for greasing the pan

3 large apples (I used Honeycrisp and Fuji)

¼ cup turbinado (raw) sugar

1½ cups all-purpose flour

½ teaspoon baking soda

¼ teaspoon kosher salt

1 teaspoon ground cinnamon

1 teaspoon ground ginger

½ teaspoon ground cloves

½ teaspoon ground allspice

¾ cup packed brown sugar

2 large eggs

1 tablespoon grated lemon zest

1 tablespoon grated peeled fresh ginger (I used a 2-inch piece and grated it with a Microplane)

1 tablespoon molasses

3 tablespoons dark rum

1 teaspoon vanilla extract

¼ cup whole milk

½ cup whole milk Greek yogurt

10 walnut halves

Vanilla ice cream or whipped cream for serving

1. Heat the oven to 350°F. Butter a 9-inch springform pan. (If you're concerned about your springform pan leaking, wrap the bottom with aluminum foil.)

2. Core and peel the apples and cut into thin slices. Melt 2 tablespoons of the butter in a large sauté pan (stainless steel works better than nonstick here) and cook until the butter is lightly browned. Add the apple slices and stir until all the slices are covered with the brown butter.

Sprinkle 2 tablespoons of the turbinado sugar over the apples and sauté, stirring occasionally, until the apples are caramelized and soft and most of the liquid has evaporated. Set aside.

3. In a medium bowl, whisk together the flour, baking soda, salt, cinnamon, ground ginger, cloves, and allspice. Set aside.

4. In the bowl of a stand mixer fitted with the paddle attachment or using a hand mixer, cream the remaining 8 tablespoons butter and the brown sugar until fluffy. Beat in the eggs. Beat in the lemon zest, grated ginger, molasses, rum, and vanilla extract. (The mixture will look curdled; it's okay.)

5. Add the flour mixture a little at a time, stirring after each addition until the batter is smooth. Fold in the milk and yogurt until they are thoroughly combined and the batter is smooth.

6. Scrape half of the batter into the prepared pan. Cover with the apple slices, then spread the other half of the batter over the apples. Smooth the top with a spatula. Arrange the walnut halves on the top of the cake and sprinkle the remaining 2 tablespoons turbinado sugar evenly over the top.

7. Bake for 50 to 60 minutes, until the top of the cake is golden brown and a tester inserted into the center comes out clean. The cake may slightly pull away from the sides of the pan. Transfer to a cooling rack, and run a knife around the edges of the cake to loosen it completely from the sides of the pan, open the ring, and remove it. Let cool completely. If you want to remove the cake from the base of the springform pan, wait until it has cooled completely, then slide a long thin spatula between the cake and the base and use a large spatula to move it to the serving plate.

8. Serve the cake as is, or with a scoop of vanilla ice cream or a blob of barely sweetened softly whipped cream.

WHAT THE COMMUNITY SAID

CHEZSUZANNE: "This was just wonderful! My five-year-old great-nephew had three pieces before we cut him off, and we caught my sister-in-law going for a fourth piece a little while ago. Huge hit, and I may make it again for a Christmas dinner party I'm having in a couple weeks."

FORTYNINER: "Thanks again, drbabs, this cake was worth every bit of all the washing up! Truly has to be one of the best cakes I have ever tasted. The combination of flavors is amazing."

LITERARY EQUIVALENT: "I made this on a lark for Thanksgiving, not even daring to promise a dessert because I hadn't made it before (and because my son is not quite four weeks old). We *love* gingerbread, have magnificent local apples (Winesaps! I caught them in season this year!), and I was so intrigued. This was instantly my hubby's favorite cake of all time, and will be made many times in the future. The crunchy top is awesome, especially for my frosting-hating hubby, and the flavors are just delicious."

MONKEYMOM: "I love the crunchy top and each bite is so interesting, with the ginger and caramelized apples. Your spice blend with the fresh ginger, lemon peel, rum is really great! I can't wait to make it again!"

TIPS AND TECHNIQUES

A&M: Eat this cake fresh, within a day.

DRBABS: "I made this yesterday for our Food52 book launch party and changed things around a bit. Since there have been questions about substitutions, I wanted to share what I did: I used apple cider in place of the rum, half-and-half instead of milk, and sour cream instead of yogurt. I also put all the liquid ingredients together in my prep and added them together in step 4, then gently stirred in the flour mixture. The cake came out delicious, but it needed about 5 to 10 more minutes of baking (it collapsed a little when it cooled, even though the tester came out dry). Turns out it's really forgiving, so feel free to make substitutions."

ABBYGAYLE: "I made it with a mixture of spelt flour and coconut flour for the wheat-intolerant in my family. It was the best dessert at our Thanksgiving meal. Only regret is that there were no leftovers."

KATJAELLEN: "Oh, this was delicious. I used apples from our last apple-picking expedition, and made it gluten free. I used King Arthur Flour gluten-free pancake mix to replace the regular flour and baking soda and, with no rum, I used apple cider. I'll definitely be making this again—probably for Thanksgiving!"

Butternut Squash and Roasted Garlic Galette

By lorinarlock / *Serves 4 to 6*

WHO: lorinarlock is a Napa, California, writer. She blogs at www.winecountrycook.com.

WHAT: A butternut squash tart that is rustic yet full of nuance.

HOW: The touch of semolina in the dough gives the delicate, buttery crust a sandy crunch, and a thyme-scented layer of ricotta and roasted garlic serves as a subtle, creamy bed for the squash.

WHY WE LOVE IT: This galette may just be our go-to first course for autumn dinner parties from now on. lorinarlock noted that it travels well too!

Pastry

¾ cup all-purpose flour

¼ cup semolina flour

½ teaspoon kosher salt

6 tablespoons chilled unsalted butter, cut into small pieces

2 to 4 tablespoons ice water

Filling

1 medium butternut squash

2 tablespoons olive oil

1 garlic clove, chopped, plus 10 cloves, unpeeled

2 teaspoons fresh thyme leaves, chopped

1 teaspoon kosher salt

½ teaspoon freshly ground black pepper

½ cup ricotta

1 cup grated fontina cheese

2 tablespoons freshly grated Parmesan cheese

1. To make the pastry: Put the flour, semolina, and salt in the bowl of a food processor and pulse to combine. Add the butter and pulse to form a mixture that looks like small peas. Add the ice water 1 tablespoon at a time, pulsing until the dough comes together, being careful not to overmix (to test, gather a bit of dough in your fingers; if it sticks together without crumbling, it's ready).

2. Transfer to a lightly floured board and shape the dough into a disk. Wrap tightly in plastic and refrigerate for at least 30 minutes, and up to 24 hours.

3. Heat the oven to 400°F. Line 2 baking sheets with parchment paper.

4. For the filling: Cut the squash into 2 pieces, separating the round part from the narrow section. Peel the squash, then cut both parts in half and remove the seeds. Cut all 4 pieces into ¼-inch-thick slices. Put the squash in a large bowl, add the olive oil, chopped garlic, and thyme, and toss to coat evenly. Spread out on one of the prepared baking sheets; set the bowl aside. Sprinkle the squash with the salt and pepper. Put the garlic cloves on the baking sheet and bake until the squash and garlic are tender, 25 to 30 minutes. Let cool. (Leave the oven on.)

5. Meanwhile, remove the dough from the refrigerator and roll it into a circle about 12 inches in diameter and ¼ inch thick. Transfer to the second parchment-lined baking sheet and refrigerate until ready to use.

6. When the garlic is cool enough to handle, peel the cloves and put them in the reserved bowl. Mash with the back of a wooden spoon until smooth. Stir in the ricotta.

7. To assemble and bake the galette: Remove the pastry from the fridge and spread the garlic-cheese mixture over it, leaving a 1-inch border. Spread the squash over the garlic-cheese mixture. Fold the edges of the dough over toward the center of the galette. Sprinkle the fontina over the center of the galette. Sprinkle the edges of the crust with the Parmesan. Bake until the crust is crisp and golden brown, 25 to 30 minutes. Let cool slightly before slicing and serving.

WHAT THE COMMUNITY SAID

WILL: "I made half of the recipe Saturday. Both my wife and I think it is quite delicious! I followed the recipe exactly, except (always an 'except') I used 100% whole wheat flour, and I cut the garlic in half for my coming-off-chemo wife's tummy. Sometimes whole wheat ruins the whole (sorry) balance, but here it fits right in."

HARDLIKEARMOUR: "I made your galette as directed and it was delicious. It's also ridiculously versatile, and the crust is perfect. I was clearing out my fridge today, and I roasted up a bunch of veggies (carrot, butternut squash, sweet potatoes, yellow pepper, red pepper, golden beets, radishes, and red onion). I made the crust, mixed some dried onion with the ricotta, spread it on, and then

piled on the veggies and cubes of Brie. I grated up the rest of my fontina and sprinkled the edges with pecorino. It came out beautifully. Thanks for such a wonderful recipe!"

TIPS AND TECHNIQUES

LORINARLOCK: "Here are some options for making the galette ahead:

1. Bake 4 to 6 hours in advance and serve at room temperature.
2. Bake for 25 minutes, without the fontina, and let sit at room temp. When you are ready to serve, sprinkle the fontina over the top and bake until the cheese is melted.
3. Assemble the galette and refrigerate for up to 24 hours, until ready to bake. The pastry may not be as crisp.
4. Bake, cool, and refrigerate overnight. Heat in a 300°F oven until warmed through. The crust won't be as crisp, but the galette still tastes great."

Crispy Delicata Rings with Currant, Fennel, and Apple Relish

By ChezSuzanne / *Serves 4*

WHO: ChezSuzanne is a San Francisco Bay Area cooking teacher. She is working to develop a series of cooking classes "to encourage locavore cooking and eating." She blogs at www.thewimpy vegetarian.com

WHAT: Rings of richly caramelized delicata squash and a zingy relish, with lime juice and zest to brighten it all and keep the sweetness in check.

HOW: "One of the many things I love about delicata squash is that you don't have to peel it," ChezSuzanne wrote. "The skin is thin and beautiful and adds to any dish you might create with it." Salting the squash helps draw out some of the moisture and allows it to brown better in the pan.

WHY WE LOVE IT: This has all the makings of a great holiday side—you can prepare its components ahead of time and not one of them is taxing. And the resulting dish is like nothing we've had before. We'll be making this one for years to come.

Delicata Rings

2 delicata squash

Salt

Olive oil

1 lime

Relish

½ cup dried currants

½ crisp apple (I used Pink Lady), peeled, cored, and cut into very small dice

1 fennel bulb, outer layer removed, trimmed, and cut into very small dice

1 cup apple cider

1 tablespoon Calvados

1. Slice the ends off the squash. Slice into ½-inch-thick rings and remove the seeds with a spoon. Lightly salt the squash and let sit for 30 minutes.

2. To make the relish: Combine all the ingredients in a small saucepan and simmer over medium heat until the cider is reduced by half. Strain. Keep warm or cool and reheat before serving.

3. Pat the squash completely dry with paper towels. Lightly coat the bottom of a sauté pan with oil and heat over medium-high heat. Lightly salt the squash rings again and add them to the pan. They should sizzle the moment they hit the pan; cook in batches and don't crowd them, or they'll steam more than they'll brown. Sauté until lightly browned, about 2 minutes per side.

4. Remove the squash rings to a serving plate, grate lime zest over them, and squeeze lime juice over them (using all the zest and juice of the lime). Scatter the relish over the crispy rings.

WHAT THE COMMUNITY SAID

MELISSAV: "Suzanne, the squash was delicious. After his first bite of squash, my husband said, 'This is delicious. What is it?' Thanks for the great recipe."

THEYEARINFOOD: "I love delicata squash precisely because you don't have to peel it! This recipe is fantastic."

TIPS AND TECHNIQUES

CHEZSUZANNE: "You can just eliminate the fennel altogether, without a substitution. (If you like, toss the seeds with some cayenne pepper, salt, and cumin, roast them in a 350°F oven, and sprinkle over the finished dish.)"

LEBURK: "Easy and delicious—my two favorite things in one recipe! I didn't have cider or currants, so I used orange juice and dried cranberries . . . mmmm . . . such a festive presentation. Thanks."

Chèvre Devils

By gingerroot / *Makes 24 stuffed dates (easily doubled)*

WHO: Read more about gingerroot and see her Roasted Radish and Potato Salad with Black Mustard and Cumin Seeds on page 9; see her recipe for Late-Night Coffee-Brined Chicken on page 201.

WHAT: Thyme-spiked chèvre and crackly spiced pecans are perfect foils for sticky-sweet Medjool dates.

HOW: After the spice- and agave-coated pecans are baked and cooled only the assembly remains: stuffing the dates with goat cheese and finishing each with a candied nut.

WHY WE LOVE IT: gingerroot wrote, "Whenever I make these, I get looks of pleasant surprise from the uninitiated, and knowing smiles from those familiar with them." Amanda says they are "thirsty-making" and therefore ideal for an open house.

Candied Pecans

2 teaspoons Chinese five-spice powder

¼ teaspoon cayenne pepper, plus more if desired

¼ cup light agave nectar

1 cup pecan halves

Sea salt

Dates

1 teaspoon dried thyme

1 teaspoon grated orange or tangerine zest

½ cup soft goat cheese, such as Montrachet, set in a bowl at room temperature to soften a bit

24 Medjool dates

1.   To make the pecans: Heat the oven to 350°F. Line a baking sheet with parchment paper.

2.   Combine the spices in a small bowl and stir to mix.

3. Put the agave nectar in a medium microwave-safe bowl and warm for 15 seconds. Add the pecans to the agave and toss to coat, then add the spices and toss to coat again. Spread the pecans in a single layer on the prepared baking sheet.

4. Bake for 10 minutes, checking and stirring once or twice with a wooden spoon. The agave should be bubbling and the pecans should be fragrant and golden brown; be careful not to burn them.

5. Remove the pan from the oven. As the pecans cool, sprinkle them with a pinch or two of sea salt, then slowly begin separating the pecans from the parchment. If they stick, let them cool a little longer. When ready, they will have a hard shell and a nice crunch.

6. To make the dates: Mix the thyme and orange zest into the softened goat cheese, stirring to combine evenly.

7. Using a sharp knife, make a slit in the top of each date and carefully remove the pit. Stuff each date with about ½ teaspoon of the goat cheese to fill the date. Top each stuffed date with a candied pecan. Arrange on a serving platter and watch them disappear!

WHAT THE COMMUNITY SAID

SUZANNE DOSSOUS-VERDIER: "I made these for a party, and while making them, I tried one. I was so blown away I didn't want to bring them to the party. Delicious!"

HARDLIKEARMOUR: "Made these last night for a party. They were amazing and got rave reviews! I wish I had leftovers, but these babies disappeared in the blink of an eye!"

TIPS AND TECHNIQUES

A&M: We liked ours packed with goat cheese and advise doubling the filling amounts if you're chèvre devils like us. You might also want to go scant on the ¼ cup of agave, to avoid runoff and concentrate the spice.

GINGERROOT: "This recipe makes more pecans than stuffed dates; store extra pecans in an airtight container, and they will keep for about a week."

FIVEANDSPICE: "I made a variation on these for my New Year's party last night, but we didn't have any thyme (shocking!), so I subbed some crushed fennel seeds and a tiny pinch of dried ginger. They were supertasty! I had a couple people who like neither dates nor goat cheese rave about them. Great party recipe!"

Variegated Spiced Latkes

By Sagegreen / *Serves 4 to 6 (makes 15 to 20 latkes)*

WHO: Sagegreen is an environmental designer and professor living in western Massachusetts.

WHAT: Deep golden latkes with a lacy, tangled appearance; the mix of sweet potato, unpeeled russets, and parsnip keeps the pancakes from being stodgy, and the fennel and fresh ginger tickle your tongue in the most pleasant of ways.

HOW: It may seem as if Sagegreen, who spent a decade perfecting her latkes, calls for an awful lot of flour, but there's no trace of that raw flour taste once these guys are fried.

WHY WE LOVE IT: These latkes are great with sour cream and applesauce, but they're also pretty addictive with nothing more than a shower of fine sea salt.

1 sweet potato, peeled

1 yellow onion

1 parsnip, peeled

2 to 3 russet potatoes
  (or Yukon Gold)

1 teaspoon kosher salt

½ teaspoon freshly ground
  black pepper

½ teaspoon freshly ground
  fennel seeds

One 1-inch-long piece (about 1 ounce),
  fresh ginger, peeled and grated

2 large eggs, beaten

⅔ cup all-purpose flour

Peanut (or other high-smoke-point) oil for pan-
  frying

Sour cream, Greek yogurt, or crème fraîche for
  serving

Applesauce, preferably homemade, for serving

1. Using the large holes on a box grater, grate the sweet potato, onion, and parsnip into a large bowl (I think hand-grating is the only way to go for these). You will need about 1 cup sweet potato and ½ cup each parsnip and onion.

2. Scrub the russet potatoes very well. Leave the skins on but remove any imperfections. Grate these into the bowl with the other vegetables; you will need about 2 cups grated russets. Add the salt, pepper, fennel, and ginger and toss well. Let rest for a few minutes.

3. Using a colander (or cheesecloth, if you prefer) wring all the excess moisture from the mix. Repeat, then return to the bowl. You can also squeeze handfuls of the mix in your hands to help remove more moisture. Mix in the beaten eggs and flour.

4. Generously coat the bottom of a heavy frying pan with peanut oil. The oil need not be deeper than ⅛ inch, if that (if you prefer thicker latkes, you might have to use up to ¼ inch of oil). Heat over medium-high heat until a drop of water added to the pan sizzles on contact.

5. Working in small batches, add ¼-cupfuls of the potato mixture to the pan to form latkes about 3 inches in diameter and about ¼ inch thick. Press down gently on the latkes with a spatula. Fry on one side until golden brown, 2 to 3 minutes, then flip and cook the other side until golden. Add more oil as necessary, trying to keep the level of oil as low as possible, but make sure the pancakes cook through—soft on the inside, crunchy on the outside. Drain on paper towels.

6. Serve warm with generous dollops of sour cream and applesauce.

TIPS AND TECHNIQUES

SAGEGREEN: "Peanut oil is best for frying these if you want that golden crunchy brown on the outside without fear of charring. If you have a peanut allergy, use a substitute oil with a high smoke point. Of course, there is always schmaltz; I probably shaved years off my life using a goose-fat version for frying while I lived in Germany, but I am staying away from that now."

MRSLARKIN: "This was dinner tonight! I realized I was out of fennel seeds halfway through the recipe, so I subbed celery seeds instead—delicious! I used my OXO potato ricer to squeeze the liquid out of the grated potatoes—works very well!"

Hanukkah Churros

By Cordelia / *Makes 20 to 25 churros*

WHO: Cordelia is a home cook who lives in Seattle.

WHAT: Light, golden shells with eggy spongelike interiors, swabbed in any of a festive trio of sauces.

HOW: An easy choux pastry is piped directly into hot oil to make free-form churros, and the dipping sauces are all quick one-pot (or bowl) affairs.

WHY WE LOVE IT: We fell in love with the concept of churros for Hanukkah—a spicy-sweet twist on the traditional *sufganiyot*, or doughnuts. Then we tasted Cordelia's version, which will make you forget every leaden state-fair churro you've ever met, and decided we needed the recipe around for the other 355 days of the year.

Churros

½ cup plus 2 tablespoons sugar

4 tablespoons unsalted butter

1 cup all-purpose flour

3 large eggs

2 teaspoons vanilla extract

2 teaspoons ground cinnamon

Vegetable oil for deep-frying (about 3 cups)

Sauces

¾ cup Nutella

¼ cup heavy cream

1½ cups frozen strawberries (or hulled fresh)

2 tablespoons sugar

1 teaspoon vanilla extract

Juice from ½ lemon

1 cup sweetened condensed milk

1. To make the churros: Put 1 cup water, 2 tablespoons of the sugar, and the butter in a small saucepan. Bring to a boil. Reduce the heat and add the flour, beating it in quickly and firmly with a whisk until a ball is formed. Take off the heat and use a wooden spoon to mix in the eggs one at a time. Stir in the vanilla extract. Let the dough cool down a bit while you make the sauces. Transfer the dough to a pastry bag fitted with a big star tip. Mix the remaining ½ cup sugar and the cinnamon together in a shallow dish.

2. To make the Nutella sauce: Warm the Nutella and the heavy cream in a bowl in the microwave for 30 seconds. Continue in 30-second intervals until the Nutella is melted. Or make it on the stove: warm the Nutella and the heavy cream in a small saucepan over medium-low heat, stirring occasionally, until smooth and melted. Mix well and serve warm.

3. To make the strawberry sauce: Put the strawberries and sugar in a small saucepan and cook over medium heat for about 10 minutes. The sugar should dissolve and the strawberries should soften and break down. Transfer the mixture to a food processor, add the vanilla and lemon juice, and process until very smooth. Set aside to cool.

4. You can serve the sweetened condensed milk as is or heat it in a saucepan over medium heat for 10 to 15 minutes, stirring constantly, until golden brown. Serve warm.

5. Heat the oil in a large heavy saucepan (the oil should be about 2 inches deep) until very hot but not smoking; to test it, add a cube of bread to the oil, it should brown in 30 seconds. Squeeze the dough into the hot oil in sections of about 4 inches. Cook 4 to 5 churros at a time, making sure not to crowd the pan. Fry the churros for 2 to 3 minutes on each side, until they puff up and turn deep golden brown. Use a slotted spoon to remove the churros from the oil and drain on paper towels. Roll the churros in the cinnamon sugar and serve immediately, with the sauces on the side.

NAKED BEET: "What a great alternative to donuts!"

TIPS AND TECHNIQUES

A&M: Cordelia uses the microwave to heat the Nutella, but our Nutella seized in the microwave. Heating it slowly on the stovetop, stirring occasionally, worked like a charm.

WINTER

Fig and Blue Cheese Savouries

By TheRunawaySpoon / *Makes about 36 hors d'oeuvres*

WHO: TheRunawaySpoon is based in Memphis, Tennessee, and blogs at www.therunawayspoon .com. She wrote, "I think I am like most people: somewhere in the middle between food snob and food schlub. Just being in the kitchen makes me happy." See her recipes for Pastitsio on page 105 and Baked Ricotta and Goat Cheese with Candied Tomatoes on page 261.

WHAT: Delicate, crumbly little thumbprints that are the perfect combination of sweet and savory— a cheese plate wrapped into one crunchy little morsel.

HOW: A simple food processor dough yields tender, buttery coins flecked with blue cheese and black pepper. Good-quality fig jam is crucial here; if you can't find one, quince or pear jam also work well.

WHY WE LOVE IT: TheRunawaySpoon came up with these as an easy hors d'oeuvre she could make on the fly when invited to friends' houses. Might we suggest that you make two batches?

1 cup all-purpose flour	4 ounces blue cheese, crumbled
8 tablespoons (1 stick) unsalted butter, at room temperature	Freshly ground black pepper
	About 3 tablespoons fig preserves

1. Heat the oven to 350°F. Line a baking sheet with parchment paper.

2. Place the flour, butter, blue cheese, and a few grinds of black pepper in the bowl of a food processor and process until the dough just comes together and starts to form a ball.

3. Dump the dough out onto a lightly floured surface and knead a few times to pull it together. Then roll out to a ⅛-inch-thick circle with a floured rolling pin. Cut rounds out of the dough with a floured 1-inch round cutter and transfer to the parchment-lined baking sheet. Reroll the scraps (no more than once) and cut more rounds.

4. Using the back of a rounded ½-teaspoon measure or your knuckle, make an indentation in the center of each dough round. Spoon about ¼ teaspoon of the fig preserves into each indentation, using your finger to push the preserves as best as possible into the indentation.

5. Bake the savouries until the preserves are bubbling and the pastry is light golden on the bottom, 10 to 12 minutes. Let cool on the baking sheet for at least 10 minutes, then remove to a wire rack to finish cooling.

WHAT THE COMMUNITY SAID

JENNIFER ANN: "I made these last night for friends and they are definitely going into heavy rotation this holiday season—so much flavor with so little effort. Thanks for a wonderful recipe!"

KAYB: "Learned something very important, making these today: Two batches is not enough!"

TIPS AND TECHNIQUES

STINKYCHEESE: "I just made these and they were fabulous. I used whole wheat pastry flour and added two ounces sharp English cheddar because I only had two ounces of blue. Love the fig jam all gooey on top."

ZINGYGINGER: "They were a tad fragile when made to ⅛-inch thickness, so I made the second batch about ⅜ to ¼ inch thick and they were much easier to pick up without falling apart in my fingers."

LMACFGREEN: "They freeze beautifully, jam and all! (Just put a little waxed paper between the layers when you pack them for the freezer.) They are the perfect thing to have on hand when you need to pull out something really good, and even better, homemade, for a yummy appetizer."

IVYG: "Scored a home run with my book club! Because I was running out of time, I chilled the dough, then rolled it out and just cut into 1-inch squares with a pizza cutter. The entire prep time was literally 5 to 10 minutes. Thank you for making me look good."

Warm Orzo Salad with Beets and Greens

By the parsley thief / *Serves 6*

WHO: the parsley thief is a stay-at-home mom, blogger, and part-time caterer in Norwalk, Connecticut. She blogs at www.parsleythief.com.

WHAT: A warm orzo salad that mingles caramelized red onions, salty bursts of feta, tender beets, woodsy greens, and crunchy toasted pine nuts.

HOW: The salad is stained fuchsia from cooking the pasta in the same tinted water as the beets, a thoughtful detail we love.

WHY WE LOVE IT: Seasonal, smart, and beautiful, this dish would look striking on a holiday buffet or alongside a handsome roasted bird.

¼ cup pine nuts	2 garlic cloves, minced
12 ounces medium beets with greens attached	8 ounces orzo
2 tablespoons extra virgin olive oil	3 ounces feta cheese, crumbled
½ medium red onion, thinly sliced	Kosher salt and freshly ground black pepper

1. Toast the pine nuts in a dry skillet over medium heat until they begin to brown. Watch carefully, as they will burn in a flash. Remove from the heat and transfer to a bowl to cool.

2. Remove the beet greens and reserve. Peel the beets and chop them into bite-size pieces. Remove the stems from the beet greens and slice the leaves into strips. Wash the greens thoroughly to remove any grit.

3. Heat the olive oil in a large skillet over medium heat. Add the red onion and garlic and cook until the onion is tender and golden brown, 10 to 15 minutes. Reduce the heat to medium-low and add the beet greens. Cover and cook, tossing occasionally, until the greens are wilted, about 5 minutes.

4. Meanwhile, cook the beets in a pot of boiling salted water until just tender, 10 to 12 minutes. Remove the beets from the pot using a slotted spoon and set aside.

5. Return the water to a boil and add the pasta. Cook until al dente; drain.

6. Transfer the orzo to a bowl, add the beets, pine nuts, beet greens, and crumbled feta, and toss. Season with salt and pepper to taste and serve.

WHAT THE COMMUNITY SAID

FUHSI: "I've made this recipe several times, and am right now making it again. The second time I strayed from the recipe, increasing the ratio of beets to orzo, but I have reverted back to being true to stated amounts, because the texture as is cannot be surpassed."

ALLIE: "This is why I love Food52—I'd never think to make something like this; it's seasonal, easy, and interesting. Thank you!"

MELISSA WHITFIELD CONWAY: "I had this the next day at a friend's, cold out of the fridge, and it was amazing! The sweet flavor of the beets and the feta were great together. I can't wait to make this for my family."

TIPS AND TECHNIQUES

PARSLEYTHIEF: "If you don't have pine nuts, slivered almonds are a great inexpensive substitute."

TAIL.FEATHERS: "Loved this! I jumped the gun and started roasting my beets before reading the boiling instruction. No biggie—I just diced and added at the end. So delish!"

BLISSFULBAKER: "Often I want to increase/decrease something in a recipe, but not here. The only substitutions I made were almonds for the pine nuts and Israeli couscous for the orzo (because that's what I had in my cupboard). Thanks for a wonderful recipe. It's a keeper!"

Warm Custard Spoon Bread

By LocalSavour / *Serves 6 to 8*

WHO: LocalSavour is based in Austin, Texas, and blogs at www.localsavour.com.

WHAT: An indulgent special-occasion breakfast that is out of this world with a drizzle of maple syrup and some crispy bacon.

HOW: An easy, two-bowl, mix-the-dry-with-the-wet approach yields a creamy, heavenly pudding.

WHY WE LOVE IT: A cross section of this layered dish reminded us of those sand jars you make in elementary school: the supple white custard center is flanked by a sunny corn bread base and a paler cap of tender white cake scented with nutmeg.

1 cup all-purpose flour	2 cups milk (I use 2%)
¾ cup stone-ground cornmeal	2 tablespoons plus 2 teaspoons unsalted butter,
2 teaspoons baking powder	melted
½ teaspoon baking soda	1½ tablespoons white vinegar
1 teaspoon freshly grated nutmeg	1 tablespoon vanilla extract
½ teaspoon sea salt	1 cup heavy cream
2 large eggs	

1. Heat the oven to 350°F. Place an ungreased 8-inch square baking dish in the oven on the middle rack to warm.

2. Mix the dry ingredients together in a large bowl.

3. In another, large bowl, whisk together the eggs, milk, 2 tablespoons of the melted butter, the vinegar, and vanilla. Add the dry ingredients and slowly stir until the batter is smooth and free of lumps.

4. Remove the heated baking dish from the oven and add the remaining 2 teaspoons butter, using a brush to coat the base and sides of the dish. Slowly scrape the batter into the dish and place it

on the oven rack. Slowly pour the cream over the batter; do not stir. Bake for 45 to 50 minutes, or until the top layer is golden brown and a knife comes out clean. Remove from the oven and let stand for 10 minutes before serving.

5. Enjoy!

WHAT THE COMMUNITY SAID

EFOOD: "I made this for brunch today, along with a root vegetable hash. It was wonderful."

LOBSTERBRIEAVOCADOBREATH: "Wow! This is a fabulous fusion of corn bread, pancake, and delicate custard delight."

BFUL: "This is scrumptious. A nice variation on the standard spoon bread recipe. I made it Christmas Eve morning. Family loved it. Served with bacon, orange juice, and freshly brewed dark coffee."

TIPS AND TECHNIQUES

MRSLARKIN: "I made this for brunch today, and since I don't own an 8-inch square baking dish, I experimented with individual straight-sided ramekins, and it works! I had a mish-mosh of sizes, but I think if you use about 10 ramekins that hold about ⅔ cup liquid, you'll have cute little rustic-looking spoon breads."

HARDLIKEARMOUR: "Made this for breakfast this A.M. Used polenta, and had to do a mix of cream and half-and-half. Came out beautifully!"

Sweet Potato and Pancetta Gratin

By cnevertz / *Serves 12*

WHO: cnevertz is based in New York City.

WHAT: Individual sweet potato gratins given a big punch of flavor from diced pancetta and Gruyère.

HOW: Use a muffin tin for easy portioning. If you choose your sweet potatoes carefully, the slices will fit perfectly into each cup to make more polished personal gratins (if you care about that sort of thing—take note, Type As!).

WHY WE LOVE IT: This is far from a "sweet" sweet potato dish. The more intense the Gruyère, the deeper the dish goes into savory territory. We say, "Bring it on!"

2 medium sweet potatoes (1 pound)

4 ounces Gruyère cheese, shredded (1 cup)

4 ounces pancetta, cut into small dice (1 cup)

¼ teaspoon salt

⅛ teaspoon freshly ground white pepper

¾ cup heavy cream

1. Heat the oven to 400°F. Generously coat a 12-cup muffin tin with butter, oil, or nonstick cooking spray.

2. Peel the sweet potatoes and slice into ⅛-inch-thick rounds. Put a slice of the sweet potato into each muffin cup. Top each with about a teaspoon of the shredded Gruyère and diced pancetta; sprinkle with a little salt and white pepper. Repeat twice, overlapping smaller sweet potato slices if necessary to make a full layer and using all the slices. Scatter the remaining cheese and pancetta on top. Spoon a tablespoon of heavy cream on top of each gratin.

3. Cover the pan loosely with a sheet of aluminum foil. Bake for 20 minutes. Remove the foil and bake, uncovered, for 20 to 25 minutes, until the sweet potatoes are tender.

4. Allow to cool for 10 minutes before removing the gratins from the muffin tin and serving.

JENNIFER ANN: "Brilliant idea! And just in time to solve my side dish dilemma for Christmas."

TIPS AND TECHNIQUES

CNEVERTZ: "Making these in muffin tins allows you to easily multiply the recipe for your guests."

VBEALE: "This is soooo delicious and easy! Great for entertaining. I substituted shallots for the pancetta to make it vegetarian. Thanks for sharing!"

Heavenly Oatmeal Molasses Rolls

By monkeymom / *Makes 12 rolls*

WHO: monkeymom is a scientist in the San Francisco Bay Area.

WHAT: Tender, rich dinner rolls, with just a hint of sweetness.

HOW: A straightforward and simple approach to bread making, no machine needed.

WHY WE LOVE IT: Chewy and full of deep flavor from the molasses, these rolls are versatile enough to complement a variety of main dishes. We love the ease of the first refrigerator rise, and these are virtually guaranteed to come out looking beautiful, with their butter-slicked and oat-flecked tops.

2 teaspoons active dry yeast

¼ cup lukewarm water

1 tablespoon dark brown sugar, plus a pinch

¾ cup whole milk

8 tablespoons (1 stick) unsalted butter, cut into cubes

¾ cup rolled oats, plus more for sprinkling

2 tablespoons molasses

2 teaspoons salt

1 large egg

2½ to 3 cups unbleached all-purpose or bread flour

2 to 3 tablespoons unsalted melted butter for brushing

Salted butter for serving

1. Combine the yeast with ¼ cup lukewarm water, and the pinch of brown sugar in a small bowl and let stand until bubbly. (If it doesn't get bubbly, throw it out and get some new yeast.)

2. Scald the milk (heat it in a small saucepan until it begins to steam and bubbles form around the edges; do not let it boil), then combine with the butter in a large bowl. When the butter has melted, add the remaining tablespoon of brown sugar, oats, molasses, and salt. Blend thoroughly and let cool to lukewarm.

3. Add the egg to the milk mixture and stir well. Add the yeast and mix to incorporate, then mix in 2½ cups flour. Add what you need to of the remaining ½ cup of flour, mixing until the dough loses its sheen. Let rest for 10 minutes.

4. Scrape the dough into a greased bowl. Turn to coat, cover with plastic wrap, and refrigerate for a minimum of 2 hours; it can sit overnight as well. It won't rise a lot.

5. Generously butter a 9-inch round cake pan. Turn the chilled dough out onto a floured work surface and knead slightly. Cut the dough into 12 pieces and shape into balls. Press each ball flat with your fingers, then roll up and tuck the edges under. Place the rolls seam side down in the buttered pan. Brush all over with half of the melted butter and sprinkle with some oats. Let rise in a warm place until doubled in size, about 2 hours.

6. Heat the oven to 350°F.

7. Bake the rolls until they are nicely browned and sound hollow when you tap their bottoms, 35 to 40 minutes. (The internal temperature, measured with an instant-read thermometer, should be 190°F.) Remove the rolls from the pan and brush generously with the remaining melted butter. Let cool on a rack for 5 to 10 minutes.

8. Serve warm, with salted butter!

WHAT THE COMMUNITY SAID

ANGEL: "There's good, and then there's, *OMG don't lose this recipe* good. This recipe is amazing. My husband, who is complimentary but never overly complimentary, couldn't stop raving about these rolls. Thank you for sharing. We loved it!"

THIRSCHFELD: "I bow to the dinner-roll goddess and the only words that fit, 'effing unbelievably wonderful'—words I once heard Daniel Patterson say to Grant Achatz."

KAYKAY: "Yeah! Congratulations. These were so delicious. How lucky am I that we live so close to each other that I get to try many of your new creations right out of the oven?! You can't ever move out of the neighborhood."

A Medley of Roasted Potatoes with Homemade Za'atar and Aleppo Pepper

By onetribegourmet / *Serves 6 to 8*

WHO: onetribegourmet is a Philadelphia-based Realtor who blogs at www.onetribegourmet.com.

WHAT: An inventive recipe that introduces za'atar, a traditional Middle Eastern spice blend, to oven-roasted potatoes.

HOW: onetribegourmet, whose recipe was inspired by a trip to Morocco and Turkey, noted that the za'atar mix can be ground, but we love the extra-crispy bites of potato that result from leaving it coarse.

WHY WE LOVE IT: This dish brings a little taste of the exotic to weekday potatoes. We're especially thrilled to have a blueprint for mixing our own za'atar to perk up just about anything, from roast chicken to scrambled eggs to a nice grilled steak.

2 to 3 pounds mixed potatoes (I used organic red and purple fingerlings and golden Buttercream potatoes), scrubbed and cut into ½-inch cubes

3 to 4 tablespoons Za'atar (recipe follows)
2 tablespoons Aleppo pepper, or to taste
Juice of 1 lemon
3 to 4 tablespoons extra virgin olive oil

1. Heat the oven to 400°F.

2. In a large bowl, mix the potatoes with the za'atar, Aleppo pepper, lemon juice, and olive oil. Spread in a single layer in a large baking dish or roasting pan. Roast the potatoes, stirring once or twice, until tender and golden brown, about 40 minutes.

Za'atar

3 tablespoons sesame seeds, toasted
2 tablespoons dried thyme

2 tablespoons ground sumac
1 tablespoon sea salt

1. Mix all the ingredients together in a small bowl. You should have about 1 cup.

WHAT THE COMMUNITY SAID

SASHA (GLOBAL TABLE ADVENTURE): "What a simple, tasty spice blend! I always say spices are the best travel souvenirs. Nice work."

TIPS AND TECHNIQUES

ONETRIBEGOURMET: "You can grind the za'atar in a coffee grinder for a finer texture. I like it coarse for this recipe."

TXDJINN: "I included the grated zest of the lemon (why let it go to waste?), which added a nice, very subtle taste to the za'atar. This is definitely a keeper. In Arabic, this recipe would be *Batata bil za'atar ou harr.*' "

A&M: Sumac is a lemony spice commonly used in Middle Eastern cuisine. Both it and Aleppo pepper, a fruity chili with a mild heat, can be found in gourmet markets.

Mulled White Wine with Pear Brandy

By merrill / *Serves 4*

WHAT: White wine infused with cardamom and star anise, as well as the more traditional triumvirate of cinnamon, ginger, and cloves, and amped up with pear brandy.

HOW: A slice of Asian pear is added to each drink as a garnish—the pear softens slightly as it absorbs the warm booze and makes for a yummy treat once you've sipped the last of the wine.

WHY WE LOVE IT: Like a delicate warm sangria, this drink is the perfect accompaniment to a cozy evening indoors.

One 750-ml bottle dry or off-dry white wine,
preferably Riesling or Grüner Veltliner

1 piece star anise

Two ¼-inch-thick slices fresh ginger

3 green cardamom pods

3 whole cloves

3 to 4 tablespoons honey, or to taste

¼ cup pear brandy, such as Poire Williams

4 slices Asian pear

1. Put the wine in a medium heavy saucepan with the star anise, ginger, cardamom, cloves, and honey (start with 3 tablespoons and adjust later if necessary). Set the pan over medium heat and bring just to a simmer, stirring occasionally. Turn off the heat and let the wine mull for at least 15 minutes.

2. Taste and add more honey if you like. Gently reheat the wine until it starts to steam, then turn off the heat and stir in the brandy.

3. Divide among 4 mugs or heatproof glasses, putting a few of the whole spices in each mug if you like, and add a slice of Asian pear. Toddy away!

MERRILL: "I'm a lightweight when it comes to booze, and I'll be the first to admit that my interpretation of a 'hot toddy' is a little loose. My husband loves *Glühwein* (German/Austrian mulled wine), but he prefers drinking white wine to red, so for this contest I decided to experiment with a mulled white wine."

DINA AVILA: "Love the spices you chose. Perfect blend of light and spicy!"

ANTONIAJAMES: "Such a fun, tasty drink! We enjoyed it with Fig and Blue Cheese Savouries (page 77) this afternoon."

HARDLIKEARMOUR: "This drink is delicious! I'm somewhat ashamed to say that my husband and I polished off an entire batch. Cheers!"

TIPS AND TECHNIQUES

MERRILL: "Any firmish pear would do nicely. I think a Bartlett would also work well."

Kentucky Hot Toddy

By Table9 / *Serves 1*

WHO: Table9 is a Greensboro, Alabama, youth program director and passionate home chef.

WHAT: A refreshing, balanced toddy that won't make you feel as if you've been hit over the head with booze.

HOW: Table9 was adamant about using Maker's Mark bourbon—"the only true bourbon to drink"—as the base of this toddy.

WHY WE LOVE IT: It turns out that bourbon and citrus are a great match, and just a hint of honey smooth out any rough edges. Cheers!

¼ cup fresh Meyer lemon juice (regular lemon juice will do in a pinch)

½ cup fresh blood orange juice

1 teaspoon honey

1 shot (1½ ounces) Maker's Mark bourbon

1 cinnamon stick

1. Combine the citrus juices with the honey and bourbon in a tumbler. Add just enough hot water to fill the glass almost to the top. Serve with the cinnamon stick.

WHAT THE COMMUNITY SAID

HARDLIKEARMOUR: "Congrats! What a beautiful drink. Love the blood orange."

Mujaddara with Spiced Yogurt

By Rivka / *Serves 4*

WHO: Rivka is a health care consultant by day, food blogger by night, and she makes a mean veggie chili. Check out her blog at www.notderbypie.com.

WHAT: A storied Middle Eastern staple with varied textures and flavors: crisp, sweet onions tangle with fluffy jasmine rice and tiny, plump French lentils that burst happily in your mouth; the minted spiced yogurt adds zip and ties everything together.

HOW: The rice and lentils are cooked and flavored separately; the magic happens when you allow them to rest together for 15 minutes before serving.

WHY WE LOVE IT: Rivka's nuanced dish is a meal all its own, and its fragrance lingers long after you've taken the last bite.

Mujaddara

¾ cup le Puy lentils (aka French lentils, the tiny dark green ones)

1 teaspoon salt

1 cup jasmine rice

2 tablespoons unsalted butter

3 tablespoons olive oil

6 cups thinly sliced onions (about 3 medium onions)

Yogurt

½ cup whole milk Greek yogurt

½ teaspoon ground cinnamon

½ teaspoon ground cumin (freshly ground if possible)

½ teaspoon ground coriander (freshly ground if possible)

½ teaspoon Aleppo pepper or hot paprika

3 tablespoons chopped fresh mint

Grated zest and juice of ½ a lemon

¼ teaspoon salt

1. To make the mujaddara: Heat the oven to 400°F.

2. Put the lentils, ½ teaspoon of the salt, and 4 cups water in a large ovenproof pot and bring to a boil. Reduce the heat and simmer the lentils until soft but not mushy, about 20 minutes. Drain and set aside. Rinse the pot.

3. Add the rice, the remaining ½ teaspoon salt, and 1½ cups water to the pot, set over medium heat, and bring to a boil. When the water begins to boil, cover the pot, transfer to the oven, and cook for 17 minutes (the tried-and-true Amanda Hesser method!), until perfectly cooked. Remove from the oven, uncover, and fluff the rice with a fork. Set aside.

4. Meanwhile, set a large deep sauté pan over medium-low heat and add the butter and 2 tablespoons of the olive oil. When the butter has mostly melted, add the onions and toss to coat with the butter and oil. After 5 minutes, the onions will soften slightly and start to release some liquid. Raise the heat to medium and cook for 10 to 12 minutes more, until the onions are very soft and browned. Add water by the tablespoon if the pan gets too dry or if the onions start to stick.

5. When the onions are well-browned, add the last tablespoon of olive oil and raise the heat to high. Cook for another 3 to 4 minutes, until the bottom layer of onions has charred and crisped; don't stir too much or the onions won't crisp up. Remove from the heat.

6. Combine the rice, lentils, and most of the onions in a large serving bowl and let sit for at least 15 minutes to marry the flavors. (Truth be told, this dish improves with age.) Taste and add more onions, if desired.

7. Meanwhile, make the yogurt: Mix all the ingredients together in a small bowl.

8. If the mujaddara has cooled significantly, reheat it in a low oven or even in the microwave for a couple of minutes. To serve, place a big scoop of mujaddara on each plate and top with a dollop of yogurt.

WHAT THE COMMUNITY SAID

SCOFF: "Anyone still wondering if they should try it: it's amazing—so much more than the sum of its parts. Rivka, you're a star."

BOULANGERE: "I love this and consider its discovery one of the high points of my year. I'm making it next week with some black Beluga lentils."

DRKATE: "Terrific! Thank you—I made this for brunch today. Honestly, this is a recipe I would want to be remembered for."

STESKER: "I love that everything in this recipe is right in my pantry. It's just about the yummiest 'meatless Monday' dish I've ever made. My two-year-old gobbles it up with gusto. And the leftovers are even better."

TIPS AND TECHNIQUES

DRBABS: "If you use oil to sauté the onions and serve the yogurt on the side, you have your vegetarian and vegan dishes all in one."

Pastitsio

By TheRunawaySpoon / *Serves 8*

WHO: Read more about TheRunawaySpoon and see her recipe for Fig and Blue Cheese Savouries on page 77; see her recipe for Baked Ricotta and Goat Cheese with Candied Tomatoes on page 261.
WHAT: Shepherd's pie meets moussaka—a lamb ragout spiced with cinnamon, oregano, sumac, and mint is blended with penne and feta and then topped with a cayenne-scented béchamel.
HOW: After a bake in the oven—we turned up the heat to 450°F for the final 10 minutes—this hearty dish emerges crisp on the perimeter with a thick toasted-béchamel cap.
WHY WE LOVE IT: We made a quadruple batch of this recipe, which was last year's Baked Pasta runner-up, for a dinner party and were reminded just how great the dish is. We immediately decided it deserved a spot in the second Food52 cookbook. It's an all-around, anytime winner.

Pastitsio

1 pound dried penne or ziti

1 tablespoon unsalted butter

2 pounds ground lamb

2 medium onions, chopped

½ cup dry red wine

One 6-ounce can tomato paste

1 teaspoon ground cinnamon

1 tablespoon dried oregano

½ teaspoon ground sumac (optional)

1 teaspoon dried mint (optional)

Salt and freshly ground black pepper

Cheese Sauce

6 tablespoons unsalted butter

½ cup all-purpose flour

3 cups whole milk

⅛ teaspoon cayenne pepper

¼ cup freshly grated Parmesan cheese

6 ounces feta cheese, crumbled

1. Cook the pasta in a large pot of boiling salted water until just al dente, about 3 minutes less than the package directions. Drain, transfer to a bowl, and stir in the butter to prevent sticking. Set aside.

2.   Meanwhile, cook the lamb in a large sauté pan over medium heat, breaking it into pieces, until no longer pink, about 8 minutes. Add the onions and cook, stirring occasionally, until soft and translucent, about 5 minutes.

3.   Transfer to a colander and shake well to drain the fat. Return the lamb and onions to the pan, add the wine, and cook over medium heat until most of the liquid has evaporated. Stir in the tomato paste, and cook for a minute. Add the cinnamon, oregano, sumac, and mint, if using, and 2 cups of water. Simmer, stirring occasionally, until thickened, 15 to 20 minutes. Season to taste with salt and pepper. Set aside to cool.

4.   To make the cheese sauce: Melt the butter in a medium saucepan over medium heat. Whisk in the flour until incorporated, about 30 seconds. Add the milk in a slow steady stream, whisking constantly so there are no lumps. Cook, whisking often, until the mixture is thick and bubbly and coats the back of a spoon, 5 to 7 minutes. Stir in the cayenne and Parmesan. Remove from the heat.

5.   Heat the oven to 350°F. Grease a 9 x 13-inch baking dish.

6.   Add the pasta to the lamb mixture and stir to combine. Toss in the feta and stir to combine. Spoon the mixture into the greased baking dish. Spread the cheese sauce over the pasta mixture, smoothing the top with the back of a spoon. Bake until browned on top in spots, 35 to 40 minutes.

7.   Remove from the oven and allow to cool for about 15 minutes before serving.

WHAT THE COMMUNITY SAID

SARASITA: "Great dish. My husband loves baked ziti, and when I made this, he went crazy for the new twist of Greek flavors, compared to the traditional Italian."

FLAWLESSMOM: "It was even better the second day. I was so happy for leftovers! Thank you for this recipe and for the suggestion of turning up the heat for the last 10 to 15 minutes. It looked exactly like the picture!"

TIPS AND TECHNIQUES

A&M: A few tips: Remember to salt the pasta water, and you should undercook the pasta because it will continue cooking in the later baking stage. When you add the tomato paste to the lamb, let it toast a bit before adding the water.

THERUNAWAYSPOON: "This can be made in one big family-style casserole, or two smaller sizes. Take one to a friend and have one for dinner."

MELISSAV: "I made everything but the cheese sauce on Sunday and put it in the fridge. When I came home from work on Monday, I whipped up the sauce and popped it in the oven. Made for a delicious and easy Monday night dinner (and lunch today)!"

ANTONIAJAMES: "Made this last night using beef instead of lamb and fresh mint, not dried. Outstanding! And so easy too."

Short Rib Ragu

By Minimally Invasive / *Serves 8 to 10*

WHO: Minimally Invasive, a graphic designer and freelance writer living in Ringwood, New Jersey, is always up for trying something new. Her latest projects are perfecting her smoker technique, as well as turning out the perfect focaccia. She blogs at www.chimeraobscura.com/mi.

WHAT: A hearty, earthy ragu best made a day in advance. We're confident this would be just as satisfying over pasta as it is over polenta.

HOW: Mushrooms, which are pureed with the rest of the sauce once the short ribs are fall-apart tender, make the liquid cloaking the shredded short ribs nice and meaty, and the wine, anchovy, tomato paste, and mustard make it sing.

WHY WE LOVE IT: Minimally Invasive wrote, "Let's be honest, short ribs are great in any incarnation, but I wanted to use them in a ragu that had a little more oomph than the typical braise, so I went into umami overdrive with porcini." The gremolata is a nice bright touch at the end. On a frosty winter evening, this would be perfect with a big green salad and the other half of that bottle of red wine.

Ragu

1 ounce dried porcini mushrooms

5 to 6 pounds short ribs

Kosher salt and freshly ground black pepper

1 tablespoon vegetable oil, bacon fat, or lard

1 large onion, chopped

2 medium carrots, peeled and chopped

2 celery stalks, chopped

2 large garlic cloves, finely chopped

2 tablespoons tomato paste

1 tablespoon anchovy paste

Half a 750-ml bottle red wine

One 14-ounce can fire-roasted tomatoes, with their juices

1 tablespoon Dijon mustard

3 to 4 dashes Worcestershire sauce

1 teaspoon dried thyme

1 teaspoon dried oregano

1 large rosemary sprig, leaves removed and chopped

2 bay leaves

4 to 5 cups chicken stock, low-sodium broth, or water

Gremolata

1 large garlic clove, minced

Grated zest of 1 large lemon

¼ cup finely chopped fresh flat-leaf parsley

½ teaspoon salt

1 teaspoon olive oil

Polenta for serving

1. To make the ragu: This is best if prepared one day before serving (see Tips and Techniques). Heat the oven to 350°F.

2. Soak the dried mushrooms in 2 cups boiling water for at least 10 minutes, until soft.

3. Meanwhile season the ribs well with salt and pepper. Heat the oil in a large ovenproof heavy pot (such as a 5-quart enameled cast iron Dutch oven) over medium heat until shimmering. Brown the ribs in batches for 2 to 3 minutes per side; set aside.

4. Pour out all but 1 tablespoon of the fat from the pot, then sauté the onion, carrots, and celery until soft. Add the garlic and stir until fragrant. Create a hot spot in the pot by moving the vegetables aside, leaving about a 3-inch circle bare. Add the tomato paste and anchovy paste to the hot spot and stir vigorously until caramelized, then stir this mixture into the vegetables. Add the red wine to deglaze the pot and cook until the liquid is reduced by half. Add the tomatoes, mustard, and Worcestershire sauce. Lift the mushrooms from the soaking liquid and add to the pot, then add the soaking liquid, minus the last ¼ inch to keep sediment out of your dish, and the herbs.

5. Add the ribs back to the pot, then add enough chicken stock so the ribs are nearly covered. Bring the liquid to a boil, then cover tightly and braise in the oven for at least 3 hours, or until the ribs are fall-apart tender.

6. Remove the ribs from the braising liquid and set aside until cool enough to handle. Meanwhile, remove the bay leaves from the braising liquid and discard. Puree the braising liquid with an immersion blender (or in batches in a regular blender, then return to the pot). Set the pot over medium-low heat to reduce if the sauce seems thin.

7. When the ribs have cooled, remove and discard the bones and any large pieces of fat. Shred the beef and return it to the pot. Let cool to room temperature, skimming any large pools of fat from the surface, and refrigerate overnight.

8. The next day, make the gremolata: Mix all the ingredients in a small bowl and let sit at room temperature for an hour before serving.

9. Remove the solidified fat from the surface of the ragu and reheat. Serve over polenta, sprinkled with the gremolata.

Hunter's-Style Chicken

By lastnightsdinner / *Serves 4 to 6*

WHO: lastnightsdinner lives in Brooklyn, New York, and describes herself as a "desk jockey by day, home cook and food blogger by night." She blogs at www.lastnightsdinner.net. See her Linguine with Sardines, Fennel, and Tomato on page 129.

WHAT: A riff on chicken cacciatore (brushing up on our culinary Italian, we learned that *cacciatore* means "hunter's-style").

HOW: A few details set this apart from other braised chicken dishes you may know: the subtle perfume of the sweet vermouth (we recommend pouring yourself a nip while the chicken simmers away), the sauce-bolstering grated carrot, and the one-two mushroom punch of dried porcini and fresh cremini.

WHY WE LOVE IT: As lastnightsdinner noted, "There's a bit of prep involved at the start, breaking down the bird, browning it in batches, soaking the dried mushrooms and sautéing the fresh, and building layers of flavor in your pot, but once everything is in the oven with its parchment cap in place, you can kick back with a Negroni and enjoy the aromas wafting your way." Serve with your favorite comfort carb—polenta, mashed potatoes, or couscous would all be happy landing pads for the rich, warming sauce and tender shreds of chicken.

One 3- to 3½-pound chicken, in pieces, or an equivalent amount of skin-on parts of your choice

Kosher or sea salt

1 cup dried porcini mushrooms

Grapeseed oil

Extra virgin olive oil

8 ounces cremini mushrooms, trimmed and quartered

¼ cup sweet (Italian/red) vermouth

2 cups chopped white or yellow onions

1 small carrot, peeled and grated (about ½ cup)

3 cups chopped ripe plum tomatoes (or an equivalent amount of canned San Marzano plum tomatoes)

1 tablespoon tomato paste, preferably double-concentrated

Pinch of red pepper flakes

1 cup dry red wine

3 tablespoons chopped fresh herbs (I used a mixture of thyme, savory, and flat-leaf parsley)

1. Heat the oven to 325°F.

2. Arrange the chicken pieces on a platter and pat dry. Season well with salt and set aside.

3. Cover the porcini with 1 cup boiling water and let steep until the mushrooms are soft, at least 10 minutes.

4. Remove the mushrooms from the soaking liquid and finely chop; strain the soaking liquid through a coffee filter to remove any grit, and set aside.

5. Heat a glug of grapeseed oil and a glug of olive oil over medium heat in a heavy ovenproof pot (such as a large enameled cast iron Dutch oven) and brown the chicken in batches, starting skin side down, until the chicken is browned and crisp-skinned. Remove the chicken pieces to a plate or platter and set aside. Pour off all but a thin layer of the rendered fat from the pot.

6. Add the cremini mushrooms to the pot, and cook, stirring occasionally, until browned on all sides. Add the chopped porcini and vermouth and cook until the liquid has evaporated. Remove the mushrooms to a bowl and set aside.

7. Add the chopped onions to the pot, along with a sprinkle of salt and a little more oil if necessary, and cook until soft and translucent. Add the carrot and stir, then add the chopped tomatoes, tomato paste, red pepper flakes, wine, and reserved mushroom liquid, stir well, and bring to a simmer.

8. Toss the chopped herbs with the mushrooms and add to the pot, stirring well. Nestle the chicken pieces on top—being sure to add any juices that have accumulated—cover the pot with a parchment lid (see Tips), and transfer the pot to the oven. Cook for at least 1 hour, preferably more, until the chicken is falling-apart tender and the sauce is thick and reduced.

WHAT THE COMMUNITY SAID

KAYB: "It's cold and ugly here in the not-sunny South, and it's supposed to snow tomorrow, and I don't care if it does, because I'm going to stay inside and make this! Great recipe, great wildcard!"

TIPS AND TECHNIQUES

LASTNIGHTSDINNER: "The parchment lid is a tip I picked up from Thomas Keller and Michael Ruhlman (from *Ad Hoc at Home* and *The Elements of Cooking*). You make a parchment lid with a circle cut out in the center to cover your braise rather than the pot lid. I haven't tried it with a stovetop braise, but it works like a dream in the oven, allowing the liquid to reduce nicely without steaming the chicken skin and losing all that nice browning you worked so hard for! It's also really easy to peek in and see how much your liquid is reducing, and add more water or whatever if needed. It's a pretty neat trick, and I've been really happy with the results."

FIVEANDSPICE: "Made this a couple of nights ago—except I used bacon for some extra umami, instead of the porcini, since I had some wonderful, smoky local bacon. It was delicious!"

EGGPLAYER: "I didn't have vermouth, so I used Marsala. It came out fabulous."

Not-Too-Virtuous Salad with Caramelized Apple Vinaigrette

By wanderash / *Serves 4 to 6*

WHO: wanderash is a mom, caterer, and writer living in Wilmette, Illinois.

WHAT: A salad that isn't wimpy or chaste, with sultry, thyme-laced caramel apple dressing and a bacony chew.

HOW: Make the most amazing salad dressing in the world and drizzle it on the salad.

WHY WE LOVE IT: For every lardon, there's a crunchy hit of celery root and a slice of fennel or tart apple. By the time you've emptied your bowl, you're sated and happy and have forgotten the chill of the outside world. The dressing recipe makes much more than you need, but you won't mind. Make more salad, or warm it gently to drizzle over a pork chop, duck breast, or anything else.

Vinaigrette

½ cup apple cider vinegar, or as needed

2 ounces brown sugar

1 Gala apple, peeled, cored, and cut into
  ¼-inch dice

1 garlic clove, minced

1 teaspoon fresh thyme leaves

Juice of ½ lemon

Salt

½ cup olive oil

¼ cup canola oil

Salad

5 slices thick-cut bacon, cut into ¼-inch lardons
  (½-inch-long strips)

4 big handfuls mixed greens (about 6 ounces)

¼ celery root, peeled and very thinly sliced or
  cut into matchsticks

1 fennel bulb, trimmed, halved, and
  very thinly sliced

¾ cup pecans, toasted

1 tart apple, cored, halved, and thinly sliced

1. To make the dressing: Combine ¼ cup plus 2 tablespoons of the vinegar and the brown sugar in a small skillet and cook over medium heat. Stir and cook until the mixture turns a dark caramel

color and begins to thicken. You will start to see big foamy bubbles on the surface. Add the apples and garlic and cook, stirring occasionally, until the apples are tender, about 5 minutes.

2. Remove from the heat and put in a blender, along with the remaining 2 tablespoons vinegar, the thyme, lemon juice, and a pinch of salt. Whoosh until blended. Then, with the motor running, slowly add the oil, blending until the dressing is emulsified. Taste and season with salt and perhaps a splash more vinegar.

3. Meanwhile, make the salad: Cook the lardons in a heavy skillet over medium heat, stirring occasionally, until crisp. Drain on a paper towel.

4. Combine the lardons and the remaining salad ingredients in a large bowl. Pour ¼ of the dressing over the salad and toss well. Taste a piece of lettuce and add more dressing if you like. (Reserve the rest of the dressing for another delicious use.)

WHAT THE COMMUNITY SAID

ANTONIAJAMES: "Wanderash, seriously, you should bottle and sell this dressing. It's one of the most delicious dressings I've ever tasted. It's so good, and it works brilliantly with so many kinds of salads."

HARDLIKEARMOUR: "I made this for dinner guests last night, and it was delicious! Great dressing, and I'm glad I've got some left in the fridge."

TIPS AND TECHNIQUES

ZOE.D: "The dressing is fantastic, and I find celery works perfectly when I don't have celery root in the house."

LACERISE: "This recipe made me rush out to buy celery root, fennel, and just the right apples. I made the dressing, cooked my lardons, and toasted the pecans in the morning so there was very little left to do to get it on the table. Getting it off the table was easy. . . . It was originally meant as a side for dinner Saturday night but ended up as our main course because we couldn't stop eating it! Dee-lish!"

Crispy Spice-Brined Pecans

By AntoniaJames / *Makes 2 cups*

WHO: AntoniaJames is a lawyer who lives in the San Francisco Bay Area. She loves cooking and is "deeply grateful for having the means to create, share with others, and eat great food" (see her Haricots Verts à la Dijonnaise on page 235).

WHAT: Spiced pecans are sitting, unassumingly, on a wonderful secret, set apart from their sugar-shellacked counterparts.

HOW: The long brining and low roasting take only time and almost no effort. But here's another secret: those times can be approximated with little ill effect.

WHY WE LOVE IT: At first glance, these nuts appear raw and untouched, but one bite betrays that they're actually perfectly salted and spiced from within, then dried to a crisp. Even when we shaved a couple hours each off the brining and roasting times, these still disappeared from the jar. The method is based on one described by Sally Fallon in *Nourishing Traditions*.

2 teaspoons sea salt

½ cinnamon stick, broken into 3 or 4 pieces

½ teaspoon ground mace

3 whole cloves

Two 3-by-1-inch strips orange peel

2 cups pecan halves

1. Combine 1½ cups boiling water with the salt, cinnamon, mace, cloves, and orange peel in a glass or ceramic bowl. Cool to lukewarm, then stir well, add the nuts, and allow them to soak for 6 to 8 hours.

2. Heat the oven to 150°F. Line a baking sheet with parchment.

3. With a slotted spoon, remove the pecans from the brining liquid and spread them on the baking sheet. Remove any whole spices and orange peel. Roast for 10 to 12 hours, stirring occasionally.

4. Enjoy!! (If by chance there are any left, store them in a tightly sealed container.)

BLISSFULBAKER: "These seem like a great gift idea!"

Roasted Fennel and White Bean Dip

By singing_baker / *Serves 12*

WHO: singing_baker is a vocal and piano instructor who has a passion for food and cooking. She lives in New York City.

WHAT: An unforgettable hors d'oeuvre that will be the star of your appetizer course.

HOW: First you roast the fennel and garlic to bring out their sugars and intensify their flavors. Then you simmer white beans in fragrant garlic-and-rosemary oil. You blend the beans and fennel with more oil so the mixture lightens and, finally, you spoon it all into a baking dish, cover it with Parmesan cheese, and slide it into a hot oven so the cheese on top toasts, leaving you with a crisp veil over the pillowy dip.

WHY WE LOVE IT: Most dips involve dumping a bunch of ingredients in a bowl and mixing them until smooth. If the ingredients are good quality, you'll end up with something worth dipping a chip into, but if you're like singing_baker and you tweak some of those ingredients, you'll end up with something divine. One bite, and you won't even remember the work that went into it.

Fennel

1 large or 2 small fennel bulbs, trimmed and cut into 1-inch pieces

2 garlic cloves, unpeeled

2 to 3 tablespoons olive oil

Salt and freshly ground black pepper

Cannellini Beans

½ cup olive oil

2 garlic cloves, minced

1 tablespoon chopped fresh rosemary

2½ cups canned cannellini beans, drained and rinsed

1 tablespoon fresh lemon juice

¼ cup olive oil

½ cup freshly grated Parmesan cheese, or more if desired

Crostini for serving

1. To make the roasted fennel: Heat the oven to 400°F.

2. Toss the fennel and garlic cloves with the olive oil and spread on a baking sheet. Season generously with salt and pepper. Roast for 30 to 40 minutes, turning twice. Let cool, then squeeze the roasted garlic out of its skin. Raise the oven temperature to 450°F.

3. To make the beans: In a small frying pan, warm the olive oil over medium heat. Add the garlic and cook until lightly golden. Add the rosemary and cannellini beans and cook for 1 minute more; be careful not to burn the garlic. Take off the heat.

4. In a food processor, combine the bean mixture, fennel, roasted garlic, lemon juice, olive oil, and 5 tablespoons of the Parmesan. Puree until smooth.

5. Transfer the puree to a small baking dish and sprinkle with the remaining 3 tablespoons cheese. Feel free to add more. If your dish is nearly full, place it on a baking sheet in case it bubbles over in the oven. Bake until the cheese is golden on top, about 15 to 20 minutes.

6. Serve with crostini. Enjoy!

WHAT THE COMMUNITY SAID

THECRABBYCOOK: "I love this. Definitely making it for the Super Bowl, although its sophisticated elements may be a little above the heads of my football cowatchers! I'll end up explaining to them what fennel is, they'll end up explaining to me who the Steelers are!"

AMYW: "Folks at the Super Bowl party LOVED this dip—adults and kids alike. It's great warm, but they loved it even at room temp. Awesome and a keeper!"

TIPS AND TECHNIQUES

BELEN_AQUINO_PERFILIO: "This dip is really yummy! We found that it gets better if you leave it overnight so the flavors can develop."

FRISSBERG: "Quick tip for those of you who like/need to make things ahead of time: I made this the night before, then transferred it to an ovenproof serving dish (without the cheese topping), covered it in foil, and baked it at 350°F for about 30 minutes (stirring every 10 minutes or so). Then I uncovered it, sprinkled on the remaining 3 tablespoons cheese, and broiled it until brown and bubbly. Worked like a charm. . . . One last tip—I had some rosemary left over, so I infused it in olive oil and then used that oil to make my crostini. Delicious!"

Tamatar Biryani (Tomato Rice)

By pauljoseph / *Serves 6*

WHO: pauljoseph lives in Kerala, India.

WHAT: A brilliant riff on regular basmati rice that comes out perfectly cooked and infused through with tomato broth.

HOW: Vary the heat of this dish by substituting other chiles (Thai chiles are much spicier than serranos) or removing the seeds and heat-packed white ribs—bear in mind that the spice will build as you eat.

WHY WE LOVE IT: This satisfying and flavorful dish is loaded with aromatics and layers of heat but easily made for a simple side or lunch. If you can't find whole mace, you can substitute ground or even skip it and let the other spices carry the dish.

1 cup Indian or Pakistani basmati rice

2 tablespoons ghee or unsalted butter

¼ teaspoon whole cloves

6 green or white cardamom pods

2 cinnamon sticks

2 blades mace or ⅛ teaspoon ground mace

1 small red onion, cut lengthwise in half and thinly sliced

1 teaspoon grated fresh ginger

4 medium garlic cloves, thinly sliced

2 to 3 fresh green Thai, cayenne, or serrano chiles (to taste), cut lengthwise into thin strips (do not remove the seeds)

One 14½-ounce can diced tomatoes

1 teaspoon kosher or coarse sea salt

¼ teaspoon ground turmeric

¼ cup finely chopped fresh cilantro (including tender stems)

1. Place the rice in a medium bowl. Fill the bowl with water to cover the rice and gently rub the slender grains through your fingers, without breaking them, to wash off any dust or light foreign objects (like loose husks), which will float to the surface. The water will become cloudy, drain off the water. Repeat three or four times, until the water remains relatively clear. Fill the bowl with cold water and let it sit at room temperature until the grains soften, 20 to 30 minutes; drain.

2. Heat the ghee in a medium saucepan over medium-high heat. Sprinkle in the cloves, cardamon pods, cinnamon sticks, and mace and cook until they sizzle, crackle, and smell aromatic, 15 to 30 seconds. Add the onion and stir-fry until light brown around the edges, 5 to 7 minutes.

3. Mix in the ginger, garlic, and chiles. Cook, stirring, for about 1 minute. (You don't want the garlic to soften and brown; its nutlike crunch is important to the rice's texture.) Stir in the tomatoes, with their juices, salt, and turmeric. Simmer, uncovered, stirring occasionally, until the tomatoes soften, 5 to 7 minutes.

4. Add the drained rice and toss gently to coat the grains with the tomato sauce. Pour in 1½ cups water and stir once to incorporate the ingredients. Bring to a boil, still over medium-high heat, and cook until the water on the surface has evaporated and craters are starting to appear in the rice, 5 to 8 minutes. Then (and not until then) stir once to bring the partially cooked layer of rice from the bottom of the pan to the surface. Cover with a tight-fitting lid, reduce the heat to the lowest-possible setting, and cook for 8 to 10 minutes. Turn off the heat and let the pan stand on the burner, undisturbed, for 10 minutes.

5. Remove the lid, fluff the rice with a fork, sprinkle with the cilantro, and serve. (Remove the cloves, cardamom pods, and cinnamon sticks before serving or just remind your guests to eat around them.)

WHAT THE COMMUNITY SAID

PANFUSINE: "Just made this for dinner (substituting crushed tomatoes for diced ones). Makes me want to quote a Sanskrit blessing: '*Anna daata sukhi bhava!* (May the person who provides you food live well and prosper!)' "

AARGERSI: "I made this for dinner last night and it was excellent—all of the seasonings are present but no one thing overpowers the other."

Linguine with Sardines, Fennel, and Tomato

By lastnightsdinner / *Serves 2 to 4*

WHO: Read more about lastnightsdinner and see her Hunter's-Style Chicken on page 113.

WHAT: A simple pantry dinner (the only thing you may have to shop for is the fennel) that packs a punch with just a few ingredients.

HOW: Perfectly al dente strands of pasta are lightly tossed in a sauce of garlic, fennel, tomato, lemon, and vermouth and studded with briny bits of sardine; the oil from the canned sardines enriches the sauce, and a shower of lemony toasted bread crumbs brightens the dish.

WHY WE LOVE IT: When we tasted this rich, sea-infused pasta dish, our first thought was, "It's amazing that you can make something that tastes this good using fish from a can!" Lastnightsdinner said she's been smitten with sardines "since my first taste (a long-ago birthday dinner at Prune in New York City, where my husband and I shared a starter of sardines with Triscuits, mustard, and cornichons)." One taste of this pasta, and you'll be smitten too.

Kosher or sea salt

1 tin (about 4¼ ounces) sardines packed in olive oil

Extra virgin olive oil

2 to 3 fat garlic cloves, smashed and roughly chopped

1 small or ½ large fennel bulb, trimmed, fronds reserved for garnish, and sliced very thin (a mandoline works great)

¼ teaspoon red pepper flakes, or more to taste

1 cup canned tomatoes, with their juice, gently crushed

¼ cup dry (French/white) vermouth

2 tablespoons lemon zest

⅓ cup toasted bread crumbs

Juice of 1 medium lemon

12 ounces linguine

1. Bring a large pot of heavily salted water to a boil. Meanwhile, open the sardine tin and drain a tablespoon or so of the oil into a wide skillet (the amount of oil in the tin will vary by brand, so add olive oil if necessary to make up a tablespoon). Warm the oil over medium-low heat, then add the garlic and cook until fragrant.

2. Add the fennel to the skillet with a sprinkle of salt, raise the heat to medium, and cook until the fennel is soft and beginning to caramelize. Add the red pepper flakes and let them sizzle for a minute, just until fragrant, then add the tomatoes with their juices. Cook until the liquid has evaporated, then add the vermouth and let that simmer briefly.

3. Meanwhile, combine 1 tablespoon of the lemon zest with the bread crumbs; set aside.

4. Add the sardines to the skillet, breaking them up slightly but leaving some chunks. Add the lemon juice to the pan. Taste and add salt if necessary.

5. Add the linguine to the boiling salted water and cook until it is just short of al dente. Using tongs, transfer the linguine to the sauce to finish cooking, adding a little bit of the starchy pasta water and tossing gently to combine. (You'll want to leave this a little wet, as the bread crumbs will soak up some of the sauce and dry the pasta out a bit when you add them.)

6. Transfer the pasta and sauce to a large warmed serving bowl (or individual pasta bowls). Add a drizzle of olive oil, sprinkle on the toasted bread crumb mixture, and garnish with the reserved fennel fronds and the remaining lemon zest.

WHAT THE COMMUNITY SAID

MIDGE: "This was a cinch to make and so, so good. Going in the pasta rotation for sure."

DEENSIEBAT: "The bread crumbs and fennel fronds totally make it—I am converted to the power of the garnish."

MONKEYMOM: "I love that this recipe can turn humble pantry items into something stellar."

PIERINO: "Damn! I love sardines as much as I love Jonathan Richman and the Modern Lovers. Great ideas at work here. I also love Prune when I can squeeze into that tiny place—I feel like a sardine."

TIPS AND TECHNIQUES

A&M: We found it challenging to caramelize the fennel without burning the garlic; if you'd like, add the garlic after you've sautéed the fennel.

LASTNIGHTSDINNER: "It goes without saying you should use the best-quality wild-caught tinned sardines you can find. Some of our favorites are Wild Planet, Cole's, MorGaDa, and BELA-Olhão, any of which work well here. Also, tiny fresh tomatoes are a wonderful replacement for canned during the summer months—Super Sweet 100s, left whole, or halved small cherry varieties work beautifully. Just add a pint or so to the pan in step 3 and let them cook until softened."

PATRICIAG: "This was so incredibly delicious! I didn't have vermouth in the house, so skipped that part. I diced a plum tomato and added that instead. Every bite had another delightful surprise. I'll make this often."

Aunt Mariah's Lemon Sponge Cups

By ENunn / *Serves 4 to 6*

WHO: ENunn is a writer living in Chicago.

WHAT: A fresh take on lemon pudding cake.

HOW: In one fell swoop, you get two desserts: a delicate, airy cake that rises to the top and browns handsomely, and a lush lemony custard that pools at the bottom, waiting for your spoon.

WHY WE LOVE IT: We're so glad ENunn unearthed her Aunt Mariah's version of classic lemon pudding cake—its evocative name, mellowed lemon pucker, and bare sweetness thoroughly won us over.

2 tablespoons unsalted butter, at room temperature

1 cup sugar

¼ cup all-purpose flour

Pinch of salt

Grated zest and juice of 1 lemon

3 large eggs, separated

1½ cups whole milk

Whipped cream for serving

1. Heat the oven to 350°F.

2. In a large bowl, cream the butter. Beat in the sugar, flour, salt, and lemon zest and juice.

3. In a small bowl, beat the egg yolks. Stir in the milk. Slowly add the second mixture to first mixture.

4. Beat the egg whites until stiff; gently fold into the batter. Pour it into ramekins or individual soufflé dishes and place in a baking pan of hot water. Bake for 45 minutes. You will have a layer of lemon custard with a gorgeous lightly browned sponge on top. Let cool a bit.

5. Turn out and serve with whipped cream, or serve in the ramekins.

MRSWHEELBARROW: "Love this recipe! It's like a lemon bar and a lemon soufflé all in one."

CHEZSUZANNE: "I just got an e-mail from one of my cousins, who lives next door to Aunt Mariah's daughter—your cousin?—and is her business partner, and just had these for dessert tonight at her home. That's gotta win a prize for 'it's a small world'! My cousin described these as luscious. Now I have to make them!"

TIPS AND TECHNIQUES

ENUNN: "Make sure you use a big fresh lemon, not some old ratty thing. You can also bake this in one large soufflé dish. Aunt Mariah likes to garnish it with a thin slice of lemon."

Clementine Pound Cake

By SavvyJulie / *Serves 10 to 12*

WHO: SavvyJulie lives in Ithaca, New York, and blogs about healthy living at www.savvyeat.com.

WHAT: A delicately spiced pound cake to bring out at teatime and dessert alike.

HOW: The recipe showcases citrus and cardamom by setting them against the backdrop of a pitch-perfect loaf cake.

WHY WE LOVE IT: The crumb is tender and melting, and the rich brown crust is as paper-thin and brittle as an eggshell, crunching pleasantly between your teeth. The perfume of the clementine zest and juice permeate the entire cake, and the cardamom (which we recommend you grind fresh) makes the party official. While this would be great with a dollop of ice cream, it certainly doesn't need it.

12 tablespoons (1½ sticks) unsalted butter, at
  room temperature, plus more for the pan

1¾ cups all-purpose flour, plus more for the pan

2 tablespoons olive oil

1¼ cups sugar

¼ cup packed light brown sugar

3 large eggs

½ teaspoon salt

1¼ teaspoons vanilla extract

1 teaspoon ground cardamom

1 tablespoon grated clementine zest (from about
  2 clementines)

¼ cup fresh clementine juice (from about 2
  clementines)

¼ cup milk

1. Heat the oven to 350°F. Butter and flour a 9 x 5 x 3-inch loaf pan.

2. In the bowl of a stand mixer fitted with the paddle attachment, or using a hand mixer in a large bowl, cream the butter, olive oil, and sugars together on medium speed until smooth and light, 3 to 5 minutes. With the mixer on medium speed, mix in the eggs one at a time until completely blended, scraping down the sides of the bowl after each addition. Beat in 1 cup of the flour, followed by the salt, vanilla, cardamom, clementine zest, and juice. Add the milk and the remaining ¾ cup flour. Beat just until the batter is smooth and consistent—do not overbeat!

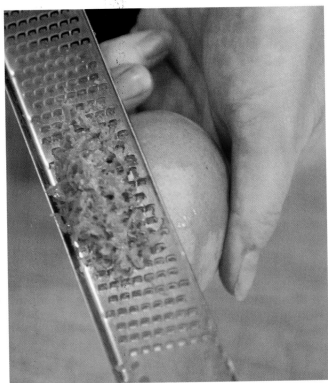

3. Scrape the batter into the prepared pan and smooth the top. Bake for 1 hour and 15 minutes, or until the edges are browned and just pulling away from the sides of the pan and a cake tester inserted in the middle of the cake comes out clean. Allow to cool for 10 minutes in the pan.

4. Run a knife or spatula around the edges of the cake to release it from the pan, and flip onto a wire rack to cool completely before slicing and serving.

WHAT THE COMMUNITY SAID

RIVKA: "Cake's in the oven now. I haven't licked this much batter in years—divine! Planning to serve with fresh strawberry compote. Very excited."

TIPS AND TECHNIQUES

SAVVYJULIE: "When you make this cake, you have to let it cool completely. All the way. It will be tough: You'll want to cut into the rich goodness immediately. You'll want to taste the citrus on your tongue, feel a bite of the cake melt in your mouth. But you must be patient. Just trust me on this one. You don't want a crumbly cake, now, do you? With this dessert, you only need a small piece. It is that rich. And that delicious. A little goes a long way."

ANTONIAJAMES: "The key to making any pound cake turn out, regardless of whether it has a chemical leavener, is to beat the butter and sugar for a good long time, until they are practically white and almost look like frosting, at the outset."

Gong Bao Ji Ding (Gong Bao Chicken)

By FrancesRenHuang / *Serves 2*

WHO: FrancesRenHuang lives in Buenos Aires. When she's not thinking about food, she is an acupuncturist and yoga teacher.

WHAT: A brilliant stir-fry that comes together in the time it takes to cook an accompanying pot of rice for dinner.

WHY WE LOVE IT: Tender morsels of chicken eagerly soak up a fragrant, velvety sauce in what is a remarkably quick and forgiving recipe. If you can't find Sichuan peppercorns, don't sweat it (you'll just miss out on their mysteriously addicting numbing quality).

½ teaspoon beaten egg

1 tablespoon plus 2 teaspoons cornstarch

Pinch of salt

1 teaspoon Chinese cooking wine

2 medium chicken thighs (3 to 4 ounces each), deboned and cut into ½-inch cubes

2 teaspoons light brown sugar

6 tablespoons chicken stock, low-sodium broth, or water

1 tablespoon Chinese black vinegar

2 teaspoons dark soy sauce

½ cup vegetable oil

8 dried red chiles, chopped

4 teaspoons Sichuan peppercorns, plus ground pepper for serving

4 garlic cloves, smashed and chopped

6 thin slices fresh ginger

2 scallions, cut into 1-inch lengths

A generous handful of peanuts

Steamed rice for serving

1. In a medium bowl, whisk together the egg, 2 teaspoons of the cornstarch, the salt, and wine. Toss with the chicken to coat, and set aside. (You can refrigerate this for up to 12 hours if you'd like.)

2. In a small bowl, stir together the brown sugar, stock, vinegar, soy sauce, and the remaining 1 tablespoon cornstarch; set aside to use for the sauce later.

3. Set a wok or large skillet over medium-high heat, add the oil, and heat until the oil is shimmering. Add half the chicken to the wok and cook, stirring frequently, until it is just half-cooked, about 2 minutes. Remove the meat with a slotted spoon and set aside on a plate. Repeat with the rest of the chicken.

4. Drain off all but 2 tablespoons of the oil from the wok. Throw in the chiles, peppercorns, garlic, ginger, and scallion and stir-fry until fragrant, about 2 minutes. Add the peanuts and stir-fry for another 1 to 2 minutes. Return the chicken to the wok and stir-fry for 2 minutes. Add the reserved sauce ingredients and simmer until the sauce thickens and the chicken is cooked through, about 3 minutes.

5. Garnish with ground Sichuan pepper and serve with rice.

WHAT THE COMMUNITY SAID

HEALTHIERKITCHEN: "I made this for dinner tonight and it was terrific! I did grind the peppercorns a little in a suribachi. . . . The sauce was perfect—a welcome change from the sickly sweet sauce found in many restaurants in the United States."

DRBABS: "Okay, so my husband sat down at the table and said, 'Wow, this smells like real Chinese food!' It was fabulous!"

TIPS AND TECHNIQUES

FRANCESRENHUANG: "Dark soy sauce is darker and thicker, contributing to a beautiful dark color and also a richer flavor, but regular soy sauce is fine as well! Feel free to use any small dried red chiles that suit you. And customize at will by adding sliced mushrooms, water chestnuts, or diced celery to the stir-fry."

Chicken That Fancies Itself Spanish, with Lemons, Onions, and Olives

By MeghanVK / *Serves 4 to 6*

WHO: MeghanVK is a television programmer living in Brooklyn, New York.

WHAT: Show-stopping chicken dinner—an oxymoron no longer!

HOW: A perfect blend of pecorino, flour, and smoked paprika coats the chicken, rendering it shaggy and crisp when browned, and the inclusion of both lemon zest and quartered lemons, plus a dash of cinnamon, lends toasty warmth.

WHY WE LOVE IT: It was the attention to detail in this cleverly adapted and absolutely delicious recipe that won us over. We found that the tenor of the smoky, tangy sauce depended on the quality of the lemons; if your lemons have a thick rind, you'll want to add just their zest and juice (as described below) to avoid a bitter sauce.

½ cup plus 1 tablespoon all-purpose flour

¼ cup freshly grated pecorino cheese

1 tablespoon smoked paprika

¼ cup olive oil

One 4-pound chicken, cut into serving pieces

Salt and freshly ground black pepper

3 medium lemons

2 large yellow onions, sliced

1 large fennel bulb, trimmed, halved, and sliced

12 garlic cloves

¾ cup pitted green olives

Pinch of ground cinnamon

1 cup canned whole tomatoes, crushed

1 cup dry white wine

1 bunch fresh cilantro, leaves and tender stems roughly chopped

1. Heat the oven to 425°F.

2. Combine ½ cup of the flour with the pecorino and 1 teaspoon of the smoked paprika in a large bowl.

3. Heat the olive oil in a large ovenproof heavy pot (such as a Dutch oven) over medium-high heat. Dry the chicken parts thoroughly with paper towels and sprinkle generously with salt

and pepper on all sides. Working in batches, dredge the chicken in the seasoned flour and add to the pot—don't crowd it! Allow the chicken to brown thoroughly about 5 minutes per side. Remove the chicken to a plate and repeat until all of the chicken pieces are golden and crispy-looking. Set the pot aside.

4. Zest one of the lemons; reserve the zest. Quarter all the lemons. (If your lemons have a thick rind, zest all 3, then juice them, discarding the rinds; this will avoid a bitter sauce.) Add the onions, quartered lemons (or the zest of 2 lemons and the juice of all 3), fennel, garlic, olives, cinammon, and the remaining 2 teaspoons smoked paprika, and the cinnamon to the pot on medium-low heat. Cook until the onions and fennel are softened, golden, and overall mushy-looking, about 10 minutes. Taste for salt. Sprinkle the mixture with the remaining tablespoon of flour and stir for 2 minutes. Add the tomatoes and wine, bring to a boil, and let bubble away for a minute or two. Add the lemon zest (or the zest of the third lemon if you are using only zest and juice).

5. Place the chicken pieces back into the pot, skin side up, along with any drippings from the plate. Poke at the onion-fennel-garlic-olive mixture until it surrounds the chicken on all sides. Bake, uncovered, for 30 minutes, or until the chicken is cooked through.

6. Garnish with the cilantro and serve. Delicious!

WHAT THE COMMUNITY SAID

SHOESTHATILIKE: "Made this for a dinner party on Friday night. *Huge* hit. It was very easy to prep and only required one pot. I will make it again!"

FRESCA: "I've made this twice this week. I never make anything twice, ever. That is how much we love this."

CHEF JAMIE B.: "This was excellent, even enjoyed as leftovers! I loved the combo of flavors, and the chicken was very tender. I served it with rice, which was a delicious pairing! I will definitely be making this again!"

TIPS AND TECHNIQUES

MEGHAN VK: "You can also try using red wine instead of white in the sauce—very different flavor!"

Creamy Potato Soup with Bacon Vinaigrette

By OB Cookie / *Serves 6*

WHO: OB Cookie is an OB/GYN resident and baby-catcher extraordinaire. She lives in Dallas, Texas, and blogs at www.obcookie.blogspot.com.

WHAT: A thick, creamy soup full of tang from a good hit of sour cream, topped with bacon.

HOW: This soup is made mostly from things that are probably sitting in your fridge right now. Is there anything better?

WHY WE LOVE IT: OB Cookie said, "I wrote this recipe when I was having a down day. Simmering homemade stock all day lifted my spirits." No wonder the recipe cheered her up! The soup on its own is a bowl of comfort, but the bacon and scallion vinaigrette really brings the dish to life. You might be wondering, as we were, about not including some of the bacon fat in the dressing, but trust us—this keeps the whole thing bright and perky. Of course, for you gluttons out there, it's always an option.

Soup

1 tablespoon unsalted butter

1 large onion, chopped

1 large carrot, peeled and chopped

1 celery stalk, chopped

3 garlic cloves, chopped

1 fresh rosemary sprig, chopped

1 teaspoon salt

6 medium russet potatoes (about 2 pounds), peeled and cut into 1-inch cubes

7 cups chicken stock, low-sodium broth, or water

1 cup low-fat sour cream

Freshly ground black pepper

Vinaigrette

4 slices thick-cut bacon

3 scallions, thinly sliced

3 tablespoons white wine vinegar

Pinch of salt

2 tablespoons extra virgin olive oil

1. To make the soup: Melt the butter in a large pot over medium-high heat. Add the onion, carrot, celery, garlic, rosemary, and salt and cook until the onions are soft, about 10 minutes.

2. Add the potatoes and stock and bring to a boil, then reduce the heat and simmer until the potatoes are very tender, about 20 minutes.

3. Remove from the heat and add the sour cream. Puree in a regular blender and return to the pot, or use an immersion blender. Add pepper to taste and keep warm.

4. To make the vinaigrette: Cook the bacon in a large skillet over medium-high heat until crisp. Drain on paper towels, then chop into small pieces.

5. In a small bowl, stir together the bacon, scallions, vinegar, and salt. Stir in the oil.

6. Serve the soup garnished with about 1 tablespoon vinaigrette per bowl.

WHAT THE COMMUNITY SAID

MRSWHEELBARROW: "Lovely idea for a soup with tang. I have every single ingredient, so it won't be long before this is on our dinner table."

FRANCESRENHUANG: "A great comfort dish for a rainy day."

ANTONIAJAMES: "Whoa!!! I'm making this! Sounds like my absolute fave, German potato salad, in a bowl!! Brilliant."

Coconut Cajeta and Chocolate Fondue

By hardlikearmour / *Makes about 2½ cups*

WHO: hardlikearmour is a veterinarian and amateur baker and cake decorator living in Portland, Oregon. See her State Fair Cream Puffs on page 257.

WHAT: A chocolate and caramel fondue, with a little coconut milk for good measure.

HOW: The silken, almost custardy fondue is punctuated with rum and vanilla, then generously salted (the way we like our caramel to be).

WHY WE LOVE IT: Not surprisingly, this fondue is gloriously rich and sweet. We found our favorite dipping instrument to be salty extra-dark pretzels. We highly recommend you try the combination.

HARDLIKEARMOUR: "This dessert fondue is inspired by a coconut dulce de leche recipe from *Bon Appétit* magazine that I found on www.epicurious.com. I've made it multiple times and have tweaked it a bit to my liking. My most major change is the addition of chocolate. It took a bit of experimenting to figure out the proportions so the chocolate doesn't overwhelm the more delicate caramel flavor. If you are not a coconut fan, don't fear—the coconuttiness is pretty subtle if you use vanilla extract and plain rum or cognac. This fondue is so luscious that you really won't believe there's no cream or butter in it. NB: This recipe can be made vegan, as long as you track down vegan turbinado sugar and use vegan dark chocolate."

Two 13½-ounce cans regular coconut milk (I use Chaokoh brand or another high-fat version)

1 cup packed light brown sugar

¾ teaspoon Diamond kosher salt (if using table salt, scale back to ½ teaspoon)

3 ounces bittersweet chocolate, finely chopped

2 teaspoons vanilla or coconut extract

3 tablespoons dark rum, coconut rum, or cognac (optional)

1. Combine the coconut milk, brown sugar, and salt in a 12-inch or larger, heavy skillet and heat over medium heat, stirring occasionally until the sugar dissolves. Increase the heat to medium-high and cook until the coconut milk is reduced and thickened, stirring more frequently as the mixture thickens; this should take 15 to 20 minutes. The mixture will become darker and the

bubbles will go from being somewhat frothy to looking more like bubbling lava. A wooden spoon or heatproof spatula scraped along the bottom from one side to another should leave a trail that "heals" within a few seconds. When this happens, remove the mixture from the heat.

2. Add the chocolate and wait about 1 minute, then stir to melt and incorporate. Once the chocolate is fully melted, stir in the vanilla and rum, if using.

3. Transfer to a fondue pot or ceramic bowl. (If you're using a fondue pot, make sure the heat is low, to prevent scorching.) Serve with fresh fruit (chunks of bananas or pineapple, strawberries, and so on), angel food or pound cake cubes, or salty pretzels.

WHAT THE COMMUNITY SAID

SPORK: "Delicious! And leftovers were great in coffee."

GREENSTUFF: "This sounds amazing! A huge increase in sophistication from the Toblerone, cream, and cognac chocolate fondue of the 1970s."

MRSLARKIN: "Oh, yes! Like a liquid Mounds bar. You could dip almonds into it, if you felt like a nut."

TIPS AND TECHNIQUES

HARDLIKEARMOUR: "If you are not a fan of chocolate, feel free to omit it. Without it, the flavor is a good balance of caramel and coconut.

"You can make the whole thing ahead, and then either put it in a microwave-safe bowl and heat at 50% for several minutes, stirring occasionally until warmed through, or put it in a metal bowl and heat over a pan of water, like a double boiler. It can be served either warm or at room temperature (has a more puddinglike texture at room temperature). I store it in a tightly sealed container in the fridge.

"I think coconut rum would also be great, especially if you're a coconut fan! I'm a huge coconut fan but am aware not everyone is. You could also go with coconut extract in place of vanilla if you wanted more coconuttiness."

Shrimp Gumbo

by drbabs / *Serves 2 to 4*

WHO: drbabs is an optometrist and food lover living in Huntington, New York. See her Ginger Apple Torte on page 51.

WHAT: A perfect weeknight gumbo featuring vegetables and plenty of meaty shrimp.

HOW: The smoky dark roux and well-chosen cocktail of spices pull in all the right flavors and kick.

WHY WE LOVE IT: drbabs, a former New Orleanian, has streamlined and lightened the Cajun classic. By design, this recipe can be made year-round from pantry staples, but you could always put a little Mardi Gras in it by adding andouille or tasso.

DRBABS WRITES: "In Louisiana, gumbo is practically religion. I wanted a lightened-up version of traditional seafood gumbo, and this is what I came up with. As with most soups, the seasonings can be adjusted according to your taste."

2 tablespoons grapeseed oil

2 tablespoons all-purpose flour

2 large onions, finely chopped

2 celery stalks, finely chopped

1 garlic clove, put through a garlic press or minced

Salt and freshly ground black pepper

1 pound medium shrimp, peeled and deveined, shells rinsed and reserved

1 cup chopped tomatoes (fresh is best, but in winter, I use Pomì chopped tomatoes)

½ teaspoon dried thyme

½ teaspoon dried oregano

½ teaspoon smoked paprika

¼ teaspoon cayenne pepper

Juice of ½ lemon

1 tablespoon Worcestershire sauce

2 tablespoons chopped fresh flat-leaf parsley

Tabasco sauce

White or brown rice for serving

1. First, make a roux: In a large cast iron Dutch oven, heat the oil over medium-low heat. Sprinkle the flour over the oil and stir until it's completely blended. Continue cooking for 5 to 10 minutes, stirring occasionally, until the roux browns and is dark caramel colored. (Be careful not to let it burn.)

2. Stir in the onions, celery, and garlic. Sprinkle in ¼ teaspoon salt and a few turns of pepper and stir well. Cover the pot and let the vegetables cook in the roux until softened, 5 to 7 minutes.

3. While the vegetables are cooking, put the shrimp shells in a medium saucepan, cover with 2 cups water, and add a good pinch of salt. (The shells should be just covered; add more water if they're not.) Bring the water to a boil, then reduce the heat to a simmer. Simmer for a couple of minutes, until the shells are bright pink. Remove from the heat.

4. Add the tomatoes, thyme, oregano, paprika, cayenne, lemon juice, and Worcestershire sauce to the vegetables in the Dutch oven. Strain the shrimp cooking liquid into the soup, stir, and let simmer, uncovered, for about 20 minutes.

5. Stir in the shrimp and let them simmer until just firm and cooked through, 3 to 5 minutes, depending on their size. Taste and adjust the seasoning.

6. Stir in the parsley and a couple of drops of Tabasco (a little goes a long way!) and serve in bowls with a large scoop of rice, and more Tabasco on the side.

WHAT THE COMMUNITY SAID

PIERINO: "Cooked a big batch up for Valentine's Day, and, yes, I did use tasso, and I did use okra and a dark roux. Got raves except for two wimpolas who only eat bland foods."

TIPS AND TECHNIQUES

ARATHI: "I made this a couple of days ago and it was excellent! I added andouille and okra and threw in some filé powder I happened to have at the end. It was so, so good! Thank you so much for the recipe, I will make this again and again."

Burnt Caramel Pudding

By Midge / *Serves 4*

WHO: Midge lives in Boston and is a journalist specializing in travel. She says, "Cooking, especially baking, is my way of winding down after a long day." See her Grown-Up Birthday Cake on page 186 and Okonomiyaki on page 229.

WHAT: A rich pudding that has just the right balance of bitter and sweet.

HOW: Starting the water bath with cool water, rather than hot, cooks the pudding very gently, giving it the most incredibly silken, glossy structure.

WHY WE LOVE IT: Puddings thickened with cornstarch make great comfort food, but Midge's luxurious caramel custard, which uses egg yolks as its only setting agent, elevates pudding to dinner-party fare. As with any egg-enriched custard, the key is careful tempering. As for the caramel, be sure to brown it as far as your nerves allow.

MIDGE SAYS: "So far, one of the best parts about living in Boston is my proximity to Toscanini's burnt caramel ice cream. I'm not even that into ice cream, but this flavor, with its slight bitter edge to cut the richness, is cracklike. I attempted to capture it in a pudding, and after incinerating a lot of sugar, I think I finally got it."

2 cups heavy cream

½ vanilla bean

½ cup sugar

3 large egg yolks, at room temperature

Fine sea salt

Whipped cream for serving

1. Heat the oven to 300°F.

2. Pour the cream into a small saucepan. Split the vanilla bean and scrape the seeds into the cream; toss the scraped pod in there too. Turn the heat to low to gently warm the cream.

3. Reserve 2 tablespoons of the sugar. Pour the remaining sugar and the 1½ tablespoons of water into a heavy-bottomed saucepan, set over medium heat, and stir until the sugar dissolves. Then crank the heat to high and let the liquid bubble away—don't stir, just swirl the pan occasionally—

until it turns dark amber. This takes about 4 minutes, but watch closely, because it happens fast. Reduce the heat to medium.

4. Moving quickly, fish the vanilla pod out of the cream (rinse it and save for another use) and slowly stir the warm cream into the caramel. Once it comes to a boil (this will happen fast), remove from the heat and let the mixture cool for about 10 minutes.

5. Whisk the egg yolks with the reserved sugar and a pinch of sea salt in a medium bowl. Whisk a little of the cream-caramel mixture into the egg yolks, then gradually whisk in the rest until it's all incorporated.

6. Strain the mixture into a pitcher or large measuring cup and pour it into four 6-ounce ramekins (see Tips and Techniques). Place the ramekins in a shallow baking pan filled halfway with cold water. If you like your caramel a bit salty, like me, sprinkle a few grains of sea salt on top of each pudding. Cook for 1 hour to 1 hour and 15 minutes, until just set.

7. Chill the puddings for at least 3 hours; but it's best if you can chill them overnight. Serve with freshly whipped cream.

WHAT THE COMMUNITY SAID

WOODSIDE: "Just the right amount of rich, and ultrasmooth and creamy. Simple, and definitely guest-worthy."

PANFUSINE: "Congratulations, Midge. . . . Such an elegant recipe, with exactly five ingredients! Awesome!"

PERFECTCHAOS: "Thank you, Midge, for this fun offering; I white-knuckled during the sugar browning, only swirling the pan now and then, but you are absolutely correct with the 4-minute time frame. All was so easy, and the custard has an amazing depth of flavor finish!"

TIPS AND TECHNIQUES

MIDGE: "I used some old custard cups that hold about 5 ounces, but 6-ounce ramekins should be fine."

Roasted Broccoli with Smoked Paprika Vinaigrette and Marcona Almonds

By arielleclementine / *Serves 2*

WHO: arielleclementine, who lives in Austin, Texas, is a stay-at-home mom and enthusiastic home cook.

WHAT: A better broccoli side dish, upgraded with the addition of smoked paprika and Marcona almonds.

HOW: Broccoli, roasted to enhance its natural sweetness, is combined with mellow sherry vinegar and the earthy, peppery bite of oil infused with smoked paprika and garlic.

WHY WE LOVE IT: arielleclementine's recipe is both easy enough to make every night and unusual enough to save for special occasions. And, in our opinion, Marcona almonds, buttery and rich, are a great addition to pretty much anything.

Broccoli

1 bunch broccoli, cut into florets	Kosher salt
Extra virgin olive oil, for drizzling	

Vinaigrette

¼ cup extra virgin olive oil	1½ tablespoons sherry vinegar
1 garlic clove, minced	Kosher salt
1 teaspoon sweet smoked paprika	¼ cup Marcona almonds

1. Heat the oven to 425°F.

2. On a large baking sheet, toss the broccoli florets with a drizzle of olive oil and a hefty sprinkling of kosher salt. Roast for 20 minutes, until brown in spots.

3. While the broccoli is roasting, make the vinaigrette: Heat the olive oil in a small skillet over medium heat until quite warm, about 2 minutes. Stir in the garlic and smoked paprika and remove the pan from the heat; let stand for 10 minutes.

4. Put the sherry vinegar and a pinch of salt in a small bowl. Slowly whisk in the paprika oil. Try to leave most of the solids (paprika and garlic) in the skillet.

5. After 20 minutes, remove the broccoli from the oven and toss the Marcona almonds on top. Drizzle with a few tablespoons of the vinaigrette, toss, and serve immediately.

SPRING

Roasted Carrot Soup

By Reeve / *Serves 4*

WHO: Reeve lives in Los Angeles.

WHAT: A simple yet complex-seeming rendition of a traditional soup.

HOW: Broil carrots to soften and sweeten them, infuse vegetable broth with fresh ginger, then whiz everything up with onions, garlic, and thyme.

WHY WE LOVE IT: It's dairy-free but supple and creamy, and roasting the carrots gives them sweet, earthy depth.

6 to 8 large carrots (about 1¾ pounds), peeled and cut into ½-inch-thick slices

¼ cup olive oil

Salt

6 cups vegetable stock, or as needed

One 1-inch-long piece fresh ginger, peeled

1 fresh thyme sprig, plus chopped thyme for garnish

½ large sweet onion, chopped

2 large garlic cloves, chopped

Freshly ground black pepper

1. Set an oven rack 6 to 8 inches from the heat source and turn on the broiler. On a large rimmed baking sheet, toss the carrots with 2 tablespoons of the olive oil and sprinkle generously with salt. Broil the carrots until they brown and soften, turning them over with a spatula every 5 minutes or so; this should take 15 to 20 minutes.

2. Meanwhile, bring the stock to a boil in a medium saucepan. Add the ginger and sprig of thyme, turn down the heat, and simmer gently for 15 minutes.

3. Just before the carrots are done put the onion in a large saucepan with the remaining 2 tablespoons olive oil and brown over medium heat, stirring frequently. Add the garlic and cook for a minute, then add the carrots.

4. Remove the ginger and thyme from the stock and add the stock to the onions and carrots. Bring to a boil and simmer for 5 to 10 minutes, until the carrots are very soft.

5. Use an immersion or a standard blender to puree the soup until smooth. If the soup seems too thick, add more stock or water and reheat gently. Add salt and pepper to taste.

6. Serve garnished with chopped thyme.

WHAT THE COMMUNITY SAID

EMILYC: "I've made many roasted vegetable soups (carrot, squash, and so on), but this one has a nice unique flavor from broiling/charring the carrots."

JSAEZ: "Simply amazing! I love how healthy, simple, and tasty it is. Thank you."

TOTALNOMS: "Thank you so much for this delicious recipe! I recently made it as my submission for my company's monthly Iron Chef competition . . . and won! The secret ingredient was ginger, so I grated some fresh ginger into the soup after blending, and it really added a great twist."

TIPS AND TECHNIQUES

A&M: We used a good-quality vegetable stock, and we recommend you do the same—since there are so few ingredients here, each one really counts.

Lamb Merguez

By MrsWheelbarrow / *Makes 1 pound bulk sausage (or a coil to serve 4)*

WHO: MrsWheelbarrow is a landscape designer in Washington, DC. She blogs at www.mrswheel barrow.com, where she hosted Charcutepalooza, a year-long charcuterie challenge in 2011.

WHAT: Homemade lamb sausage, perfectly spiced and perfumed with a custom spice blend.

HOW: No need to fuss with casings here: you just mix, make patties, and fry them up.

WHY WE LOVE IT: This recipe reminded us how simple making your own sausage can be. And these are so good—ready to join poached eggs and toast or get stuffed into a pita with tzatziki and fresh veggies.

1 pound freshly ground lamb shoulder
2 garlic cloves, finely minced
1 teaspoon grated fresh ginger
1 tablespoon Spice Mixture
   (recipe follows)

2 tablespoons harissa (I prefer fresh harissa, as opposed to what is available in a can or a tube)
1 tablespoon tomato paste
Ice water as needed
¼ teaspoon salt, or more to taste

1. Combine all the ingredients except the ice water and salt in the bowl of a stand mixer fitted with the paddle attachment and mix on low speed. Add ice water a tablespoon at a time, mixing until the mixture is well combined. Add salt. (If you have ground the meat yourself, you probably won't need much ice water.)

2. Form a little patty of the mixture and cook it in a small frying pan over medium-high heat. Taste the patty and adjust the seasoning as you see fit.

3. Cover the mixture and refrigerate for at least an hour, preferably overnight, to help the flavors develop.

4. Dip your hands in ice water as you form sausage patties, about 2 inches in diameter and ½ inch thick. Refrigerate the patties if you are not going to cook them right away. (Or, if you like, you can stuff the sausage mixture into a casing to form a long coil.)

5. Fry the patties in a heavy frying pan over medium-high heat for 3 to 4 minutes per side until browned. (Or grill the merguez coil for 10 to 12 minutes, turning once.)

Spice Mixture

1 tablespoon coriander seeds, toasted

1 tablespoon cumin seeds, toasted

1 tablespoon anise seeds (or fennel seeds in a pinch), toasted

1 tablespoon ground cinnamon (I used Ceylon)

½ to 1 teaspoon cayenne pepper, depending on the spiciness of your harissa

2 teaspoons turmeric

1. Combine all the ingredients and finely grind using a spice grinder or a mortar and pestle. The extra can be stored in a lidded glass jar.

WHAT THE COMMUNITY SAID

CREAMTEA: "I made a big batch of these for a luncheon yesterday, and they were a big hit. I seasoned them with Aleppo pepper instead of cayenne. One guest couldn't stop eating them! Fortunately there are two patties left over for a midnight nibble—don't tell."

BELLA S.F.: "This was really wonderful! I am so looking forward to having the merguez again tonight. You really do need to let it sit for a day to let the flavors infuse."

TIPS AND TECHNIQUES

A&M: Since harissa brands can vary, we recommend starting with the minimum amount of cayenne and salt in the sausage and searing off a patty to taste test (lucky you!).

MRSWHEELBARROW: "Merguez is traditionally made with lamb. More specifically, it's made without added fat, so it's the leanest sausage I know. I did try making it with goat and thought it was great, but leg of lamb is a little lean for the sausage. Shoulder is the best cut—actually, neck! If you're not grinding it yourself, ask the butcher to grind up lamb stew meat. They make a spectacular dinner party offering with lentils de Puy, crusty bread, and a green salad with figs and Marcona almonds."

Tangerine and Almond Shortbread Tart

By lorigoldsby / *Serves 12*

WHO: lorigoldsby lives in Fishers, Iowa. She made this winning tart recipe on *The Martha Stewart Show*.

WHAT: Reminiscent of a big, chewy, fragrant Florentine cookie tucked into a rich, buttery crust.

HOW: Make a press-in shortbread crust, fill it with a fragrant caramel filling chock-full of sliced almonds, and bake!

WHY WE LOVE IT: Lori's technique of applying judicious amounts of juice and/or zest to all of the components ensures a decidedly tangerine-flavored tart.

Tart

2 tangerines

1¾ cups all-purpose flour

⅓ cup confectioners' sugar

1 teaspoon kosher salt

12 tablespoons (1½ sticks) chilled unsalted
  butter, diced

½ cup superfine sugar

¼ cup packed dark brown sugar

¼ cup orange blossom honey

1 cup heavy cream

3 cups sliced almonds, toasted

Optional Garnish

1 cup heavy cream

½ teaspoon vanilla extract

1 tablespoon superfine sugar

Small fresh mint sprigs

1. Zest the tangerines and juice them. Chill the juice.

2. Pulse the flour, confectioners' sugar, salt, butter, and tangerine zest in the bowl of a food processor until combined and the butter pieces are pea-size. Add tangerine juice by the tablespoon, pulsing, until the dough looks like wet sand (reserve the remaining juice). Pulse just until the dough starts to form a ball.

3. Line the bottom of a 10-inch tart pan with a removable base with buttered parchment paper. Pat the dough into the tart pan, being careful to press it up and into the sides. Chill the crust for at least 1 hour, and up to 4.

4. Heat the oven to 375°F.

5. In a heavy saucepan, mix together the superfine sugar, brown sugar, honey, and 2 teaspoons of the reserved tangerine juice and cook over medium-low heat, swirling the pan gently, until the sugars and honey dissolve, then cook for 5 to 7 minutes, until the mixture darkens and caramelizes. (Tip: You can use the leftover tangerine juice mixed with some warm water to brush down the sides of the pan to remove any sugar crystals.)

6. Add the cream, increase the heat to medium, and cook the mixture at a low boil for 8 to 10 minutes, until it is richly caramelized and thick, making sure it doesn't boil over. Stir in the almonds and spread the mixture in the chilled tart crust.

7. Bake the tart for 30 minutes, then lower the temperature to 350°F and bake for another 15 minutes, or until the crust is richly browned. Cool the tart completely on a rack.

8. To make the optional whipped cream: Whip the cream, vanilla, and sugar together.

9. To serve, remove the sides of the pan and, using a long-bladed spatula, slide the tart off the pan bottom and onto a cake stand or platter. Serve with sweetened whipped cream and a mint garnish.

WHAT THE COMMUNITY SAID

A&M: Don't be intimidated by the huge pile of almonds you're instructed to toast—they fit perfectly in our 10-inch tart shell.

STEVEMR: "Came out perfectly, and looked beautiful too. Didn't last long, though. The 'one-more-thin-slice' gremlin decimated it quickly."

TIPS AND TECHNIQUES

LORIGOLDSBY: "I use superfine sugar out of habit when making caramel or candies. It melts so much more easily, without you having to worry about a grainy texture."

Roasted Butterflied Chicken with Cardamom and Yogurt

By TasteFood / *Serves 2 to 4*

WHO: TasteFood resides in the San Francisco Bay Area and blogs at www.tastefoodblog.com. She studied at Le Cordon Bleu and lived in Europe with her family for seventeen years.

WHAT: An everyday roast chicken turned on its head.

HOW: Bathe the bird in a spiced yogurt marinade, butterfly it, and flatten it into a cast iron skillet to roast.

WHY WE LOVE IT: The incomparably crispy skin is brightened by the fragrant rub, a testament to the benefits of grinding whole spices—you get so much more flavor and aroma.

Seeds from 6 cardamom pods

1 teaspoon black peppercorns

2 teaspoons sea salt

1 teaspoon freshly ground coriander

1 teaspoon freshly ground cumin

3 garlic cloves

1 tablespoon olive oil

½ cup whole milk yogurt

1 tablespoon grated fresh ginger

1 tablespoon fresh lemon juice

One 3- to 4-pound chicken, butterflied

Fresh cilantro leaves for garnish

1. Grind the cardamom seeds and peppercorns to a fine powder in a mortar and pestle or a spice/coffee grinder. Stir in the salt, coriander, and cumin, then add the garlic and smash it. Add the olive oil and work everything together to form a paste. Transfer to a small bowl and stir in the yogurt, ginger, and lemon juice.

2. Place the chicken in a large bowl or a baking dish. Rub about half the yogurt mixture between the skin and the meat over the breasts and thighs. Then smear the remaining yogurt all over the chicken, front and back. Refrigerate for at least 3 hours, and up to 24 hours.

3. Thirty minutes before roasting, remove the chicken from the refrigerator and let it sit at room temperature. Heat the oven to 425°F.

4. Place the chicken breast side up in a cast iron skillet or baking pan. Roast for 45 minutes to 1 hour, until the internal temperature of the thickest part of the thigh registers 165°F. Let the chicken rest for 15 minutes before carving.

5. Serve the chicken garnished with cilantro leaves.

WHAT THE COMMUNITY SAID

COOKBOOKCHICK: "The juices from the pan are wonderful over rice."

EMILYC: "I made this tonight for the first time and absolutely loved it! The marinade is full of flavor and is well balanced—and it's great to be able to fully prep the chicken the night before. I'll be making this again and again!"

TIPS AND TECHNIQUES

A&M: If you have only 3 hours to marinate, that'll do, but in our experience, overnight is well worth the wait. Depending on your oven, you might need to cover the chicken with foil for the last 15 minutes of cooking if it's getting too brown.

AMANDA: "My easy method for butterflying a chicken: Using poultry shears, cut the backbone out of the chicken. Turn the chicken skin-side up and press down on the breast bone to flatten the chicken."

Louisa's Cake

By SML Office / *Serves 6*

WHO: SML Office is an American art director and graphic designer living in Zurich.

WHAT: An airy, lightly sweet cake suited equally to breakfast and dessert.

HOW: Ricotta, eggs, and plenty of butter give the cake richness, grated apple lends heft, and lemon zest keeps things zippy.

WHY WE LOVE IT: SML Office got the recipe for this cake from Louisa, a family friend in Chianti, and no wonder: only a true Italian *nonna* could produce something this ethereal from such a simple list of ingredients.

9 tablespoons unsalted butter, at room temperature, plus more for the pan

1¼ cups all-purpose flour, plus more for the pan

1 cup plus 2 tablespoons sugar

3 large eggs

Pinch of salt

1 cup fresh ricotta

Grated zest of 1 lemon

1 tablespoon baking powder

1 apple, peeled, cored, and grated (should yield about 1 cup)

Confectioners' sugar for dusting (optional)

1. Heat the oven to 400°F. Butter and flour a 9- or 10-inch springform pan.

2. In the bowl of a stand mixer fitted with the paddle attachment, cream the butter and sugar on medium speed until light and fluffy, 3 to 5 minutes. With the mixer on the lowest speed, add the eggs one at a time, mixing well after each addition. Add the flour, then add the salt, ricotta, lemon zest, baking powder, and apple, mixing well after each addition.

3. Scrape the batter into the prepared pan and smooth the top. Bake for 25 to 35 minutes, until the cake is golden brown and is starting to pull away from the sides of the pan. Cool in the pan on a wire rack for 10 minutes.

4. Turn the cake out of the pan and cool completely on the rack.

5. Sift confectioners' sugar over the top of the cake and/or serve with your favorite seasonal fruit.

WHAT THE COMMUNITY SAID

LOUISA: "I made this cake last week—doubled the recipe and baked it in a Bundt pan. It looked and tasted wonderful and was fragrant and delicious. Everybody loved it, and it was even better the second and third day."

PHINNEYCOOK: "This is a great cake! Beautiful, dense, moist, and the perfect foil for a fruit topping, either fresh or compote. I served it last night with fresh figs . . . perfect."

RYANBISSOON: "Such a simple, elegant, and delicious cake. It's excellent just on its own, but I've also used it as the layers for a strawberry shortcake. Amazing!"

Grandma DiLaura's Ricotta Gnocchi

By cdilaura / *Serves 4*

WHO: cdilaura now works at Food52 and blogs at www.8ateATeight.com.

WHAT: Foolproof homemade gnocchi, perfect for a weeknight dinner.

HOW: Mix, shape, boil, and dinner's on the table in a flash.

WHY WE LOVE IT: These light ricotta dumplings won't weigh you down like their potato-based counterparts. We love them nearly bare—just tossed in some brown butter—so you really taste the ricotta and speckles of nutmeg.

1 pound fresh whole milk ricotta

1 large egg

1 tablespoon olive oil

¼ cup finely grated Parmesan cheese, plus more
    for serving

Freshly grated nutmeg

2 cups all-purpose flour, sifted, plus more for
    rolling the dough

Salt

Browned butter or other sauce of your choice

1. In a large bowl, mix together the ricotta, egg, and olive oil. Add the Parmesan and a few sprinkles of nutmeg to taste. Add the flour a little at a time, stirring until the dough comes together.

2. Dump the dough out onto a generously floured surface and work it with your hands to bring it together into a ball. Add more flour as necessary until the dough is smooth and no longer sticks to your hands.

3. Cut slices of dough as if you're cutting a loaf of bread and roll each one into a rope about as thick as your thumb by spreading your hands and fingers and rolling from the center out to the ends of the rope.

4. Line up 2 ropes parallel to one another and cut them into 1-inch pieces. Gently roll a piece down the back of a fork to make an impression in the gnocchi to help hold the sauce, and transfer to a lightly floured or nonstick baking sheet. Repeat with the remaining pieces, then put them in

the freezer while you make the rest of the gnocchi. (If you plan to save any gnocchi for future use, allow them to freeze entirely on the baking sheet, then store in a zip-top bag.)

5. When you're ready to cook the gnocchi, bring a large pot of generously salted water to a boil over high heat. Add the gnocchi to the boiling water in batches and gently stir once with a wooden spoon to create movement and prevent the gnocchi from sticking to the bottom of the pot. As they rise to the top (a sign they are cooked), scoop them out with a strainer or a wire skimmer and place in a warm serving bowl, shaking off the excess water.

6. To serve, gently toss the gnocchi in brown butter (or other sauce) in a large sauté pan, and return to the serving bowl. (Alternatively, scoop some warm sauce on top of each layer of gnocchi as you place them in the bowl to eliminate the need to stir them with the sauce at the end and risk damaging or smashing them.) Sprinkle grated Parmesan generously over the top and serve.

WHAT THE COMMUNITY SAID

CURIOUSANYONE: "So bloody easy to make. You'll never make the potato version again! Easily something that could be made on a weeknight, no problem. I served mine with roasted mushrooms and white truffle butter."

SPAETZLEGIRL: "I made these last night, and the thrill of eating one's own homemade gnocchi should not be underestimated. Great recipe; I have a feeling I'll be doing these again and again."

TIPS AND TECHNIQUES

CDILAURA: "Freezing the gnocchi is not necessary if you're cooking them right away, but it does help prevent them from sticking together when you add them to the water. All you really need is about 10 to 15 minutes to give them a chance to firm up on the outside before dropping them in the pot."

Flamin' Cajun Shrimp

By fiveandspice / *Serves 2 to 4*

WHO: fiveandspice is a grad student in food policy and a self-dubbed Renaissance woman living in Boston.

WHAT: Tender, garlicky shrimp that skew more toward gumbo than other boozy shrimp dishes like scampi.

HOW: The shrimp get a quick marinade of herbs and spices before they are cooked in a wash of butter, garlic, shallot, lemon juice, and Worcestershire. A generous hit of cognac, a quick flame job, and another swirl of butter finish off the dish.

WHY WE LOVE IT: The Worcestershire and paprika give the sauce an earthy quality, while the cognac envelops the shrimp like a warm, sweet blanket. And we love any recipe that embraces the ritual of peel-and-eat.

25 to 30 large shrimp (3 to 4 pounds) in the shell
 (though this also works with peeled shrimp, if
 you must)
1 teaspoon sweet paprika
¾ teaspoon freshly ground black pepper
½ teaspoon salt
¼ teaspoon dried oregano
⅛ teaspoon dried thyme
⅛ teaspoon cayenne pepper

Grated zest of ½ lemon
5 tablespoons unsalted butter, cut into chunks
4 garlic cloves, finely minced
1 tablespoon minced shallot
3 tablespoons fresh lemon juice
3 tablespoons Worcestershire sauce
¼ cup cognac or other brandy
French bread for serving

1. In a large bowl, combine the shrimp with the paprika, pepper, salt, oregano, thyme, cayenne, and lemon zest and toss to coat well.

2. In a large frying pan, heat 2 tablespoons of the butter over medium-high heat until foaming. Stir in the garlic, shallot, lemon juice, and Worcestershire sauce and sauté for 2 to 3 minutes,

until the garlic and shallot have softened. Add the shrimp and sauté until just turning pink, about 3 minutes.

3. Carefully tilt the pan away from you, pour in the cognac with a ladle, and use a long match or a long-handled lighter to light the cognac, then let it blaze out—this should take only 15 seconds or so. (I once had a friend add way too much cognac to a flambé and the fire just kept going and going—if this happens, please just blow it out!)

4. Take the pan off the heat and stir in the remaining 3 tablespoons butter until it melts. Serve with lots of crusty French bread, a big green salad (heck, why not eat that with your fingers too?), and some cold beer.

WHAT THE COMMUNITY SAID

FIVEANDSPICE: "Actually, I think the spicing of these shrimp is a little more Creole than Cajun, but that doesn't make a slant rhyme with flamin', now does it? You can use peeled shrimp, but I really recommend shell-on shrimp because the shrimp meat cooks to a nicer texture, while the sauce also winds up with better flavor."

BRICKSOJ: "Made this over the weekend for a dinner party—amazing. The best part was sopping up the sauce with warm French bread. Will definitely add into heavy rotation in my kitchen!"

LORIGOLDSBY: "We make a very similar dish with dark beer—but, like a fool, I've been peeling the shrimp for everyone!"

Grown-Up Birthday Cake

By Midge / *Makes enough for a birthday party (serves 8 to 10)*

WHO: Read more about Midge and see her recipe for Burnt Caramel Pudding on page 155; see her recipe for Okonomiyaki on page 229.

WHAT: A sweet spongy cake filled with jam and iced with a rich chocolate buttercream.

HOW: Make a classic two-layer sponge cake, adding white wine and olive oil to the batter, then quickly assemble with jam and a chocolate icing.

WHY WE LOVE IT: Olive oil and wine make the cake fruity and complex (do use good ones, as you'll taste all of their delicious nuances); the jam layer swings in with a little flash and tartness; and the thin coat of creamy chocolate icing seals the deal.

Cake

Butter for the pans

2½ cups all-purpose flour, plus more for the pans

½ teaspoon salt

1 tablespoon baking soda

2 cups sugar

4 large eggs

1 teaspoon vanilla extract

1 cup dry white wine

1 cup olive oil

1 cup raspberry jam (preferably homemade, of course, but I use Bonne Maman)

Chocolate Buttercream Icing

8 tablespoons (1 stick) unsalted butter, at room temperature

1 cup confectioners' sugar

½ cup Dutch-processed cocoa powder

¼ cup whole milk

1 teaspoon vanilla extract

1. To make the cake: Heat the oven to 350°F. Butter and lightly flour two 9-inch round cake pans.

2. Sift the flour, salt, and baking soda into a bowl. Set aside.

3. In the bowl of a stand mixer fitted with the paddle attachment, beat the sugar and eggs on medium-high speed for a minute. On low speed, mix in the vanilla, wine, and oil. Remove the bowl from the mixer stand and, using a rubber spatula, gently fold the dry ingredients into the batter just until smooth.

4. Pour the batter into the prepared pans. Bake for 25 to 30 minutes, until a cake tester inserted in the center comes out clean. Cool the cakes in the pans on wire racks.

5. To make the icing: Using a stand mixer or a hand mixer, cream together the butter and sugar until light and fluffy. Mix in the cocoa powder, then gradually add the milk, beating until it looks like icing. Mix in the vanilla.

6. To assemble the cake: Spread a layer of jam over the top of one of the layers, then top with the other layer. Frost the top with the icing.

WHAT THE COMMUNITY SAID

MIDGE: "I've used reasonably priced Grüner Veltliner and French Sauvignon Blanc. My sister likes to use Chardonnay. Really, whatever you like to drink and have on hand!"

FRAN MCGINTY: "Made this but used an orange olive oil. I didn't know how it would work with the wine, but it was fabulous! The orange and chocolate went very well together. I made the chocolate frosting and added some grated orange zest to it. I used apricot jam. I am going to have fun playing with this one."

TIPS AND TECHNIQUES

A&M: Line your cake pans with parchment circles to make sure the layers turn out without a hitch. And if you run into any trouble with lumps in the icing, just whisk like mad till it smooths out.

Herbed Beef Skewers with Horseradish Cream

By Oui, Chef / Serves 2 to 3

WHO: Read more about Oui, Chef and see his recipe for Roasted Red Pepper Soup with Corn and Cilantro on page 5.

WHAT: A clever riff on the traditional Sunday rib roast.

HOW: Marinated sirloin strips are threaded onto rosemary sprigs before meeting up with a hot grill pan. While the steak marinates, you whip up a bright, creamy horseradish sauce.

WHY WE LOVE IT: These sirloin roll-ups are tender and succulent, and the rosemary skewers make for a pretty sensational presentation; the horseradish cream is both tangy and lush.

Marinade

2 tablespoons Dijon mustard

2 garlic cloves, minced

1 tablespoon soy sauce

1 teaspoon minced fresh thyme

⅛ teaspoon pimentón (sweet smoked paprika)

⅓ cup extra virgin olive oil

Horseradish Cream

½ cup crème fraîche

2 tablespoons heavy cream

2 to 3 tablespoons prepared horseradish
   (to taste)

Finely grated zest of 1 lemon

Kosher salt and freshly ground black pepper

A few pink peppercorns (optional)

Beef Skewers

1 sirloin steak (3 to 4 pounds),
   about 1½ inches thick

3 long, sturdy rosemary sprigs (or metal skewers)

About 12 large fresh basil leaves

Canola oil

Maldon salt or fleur de sel

1. To make the marinade: Whisk together the mustard, garlic, soy sauce, thyme, pimentón, and olive oil in a bowl. Set aside. (This will make enough marinade for 2 steaks.)

2. To make the horseradish cream: Whisk together the crème fraîche, cream, horseradish, and lemon zest. Season to taste with salt and pepper. Sprinkle with a few pink peppercorns if you have them. Cover and refrigerate until ready to serve.

3. Slice the sirloin against the grain into ⅛-inch-thick planks (it helps to throw the steak into the freezer to firm up for 45 minutes to 1 hour before you attempt to slice it this thin). Brush each slice of steak on both sides with the marinade and place on a platter. Cover and refrigerate for 1 hour. (Reserve the remaining marinade for another use.)

4. Prep the rosemary skewers by pulling off the lower leaves and sharpening the naked ends of the sprigs with a paring knife. Lay the marinated steak strips on a cutting board and top each with a fresh basil leaf. Roll up tightly and skewer onto the rosemary sprigs, leaving some breathing room between each roll. Wrap the exposed rosemary leaves in aluminum foil to keep them from getting totally charred when you cook the skewers.

5. Heat a grill pan over high heat, and when it is very hot, coat with a thin layer of canola oil. Lay the skewers in the pan with the foiled ends hanging out, lower the heat a touch, press the meat down against the pan with tongs, and cook for 1½ to 2 minutes per side, flipping once.

6. Remove the skewers to a cutting board, sprinkle lightly with Maldon salt, and serve with the horseradish cream.

WHAT THE COMMUNITY SAID

LASTNIGHTSDINNER: "My husband made these Saturday night, and we loved them. I was scooping up that horseradish cream with the beef, my roasted potatoes, and, yes, my fingers! What a great dish."

TIPS AND TECHNIQUES

A&M: It's up to you and your taste buds, but we used the maximum amount of horseradish. Because that's how we roll.

OUI, CHEF: "I cooked mine on a gas cooktop in a Le Creuset grill pan, though I'm sure they would be fine on an outdoor grill if that is what you choose. I found that at 1½ minutes per side, the inside was nicely medium-rare but the outside wasn't overdone. Slicing the meat thin and against the grain helps the outer layer of the roll maintain a tender feel, even though it does cook more. You may want to cook a lone roll with a toothpick through it first, to get the timing right."

Afghan Dumplings with
Lamb Kofta and Yogurt Sauce

By Katie Morford and Humaira Ghilzai / *Serves 5*

WHO: Katie is a food and nutrition writer who blogs at www.momskitchenhandbook.com; Humaira is a cultural consultant and founder of Afghan Friends Network. Together they write the blog www.afghancooking.net.

WHAT: An Afghan dish (known as *aushak*) much like a meaty ravioli, only deconstructed.

HOW: Wonton wrappers are filled with a sharp, peppery scallion paste, and then both a cooling yogurt sauce and a warmly spiced tomato lamb ragu are spooned across the top.

WHY WE LOVE IT: According to Katie and Humaira, "*Aushak* is traditionally made in community: Families gather and assemble the dumplings." The magical part? All of the pieces come together swiftly, so then you can all sit down and enjoy each other's company.

Dumplings and Kofta

¼ cup extra virgin olive oil

1 large yellow onion, finely chopped

2 garlic cloves, minced

1 pound ground lamb

1 cup tomato sauce

2½ teaspoons kosher salt

1½ teaspoons sweet paprika

1½ teaspoons ground coriander

½ teaspoon freshly ground black pepper

1 pound scallions

½ teaspoon red pepper flakes

About 25 wonton wrappers

1 teaspoon white vinegar

Sauce

1 cup plain whole milk yogurt

½ teaspoon dried ground granulated garlic

½ teaspoon kosher salt

1 tablespoon dried mint

1. In a large sauté pan, heat 3 tablespoons of the olive oil over medium heat. Add the onion and sauté until tender and translucent, 3 to 5 minutes. Add the garlic and sauté for another minute. Add the lamb and sauté until cooked through, breaking up the lumps with the back of a spoon.

Add the tomato sauce, 1½ teaspoons of the salt, the paprika, coriander, and pepper and cook over low heat, stirring regularly, for 20 minutes. Set aside.

2. While the meat is cooking, trim the root ends off the scallions and finely chop them, including both white and dark green parts; a food processor is useful here. Heat the remaining tablespoon of olive oil in a large sauté pan over medium heat. Add the scallions, the remaining 1 teaspoon salt, and the red pepper flakes, turn the heat to low, and cook until the scallions are tender, about 10 minutes. Set aside, covered, and keep warm.

3. To assemble the dumplings: Fill a small bowl with water and put it at your work station. Set a wonton wrapper on your work surface, dip your finger into the water, and moisten the edges of two connecting sides of the wrapper (the water will serve as glue for the dumpling). Put about a teaspoon of sautéed scallions in the center of the wrapper. Fold the dough over in the shape of a triangle and use the tip of your finger to firmly press the edges of the dough together to form a tight seal. Next, lift the two longest points of the triangle, moisten them and press them together, creating a little circle over the dumpling (it will look like a fancy napkin fold). Repeat with the remaining wrappers.

4. Meanwhile, bring a large pot of water to a gentle boil.

5. Add the vinegar to the boiling water, then add the dumplings and boil until the wontons are tender, about 4 minutes.

6. While the dumplings are cooking, make the sauce: Stir together the yogurt, dried garlic, and salt in a bowl.

7. Gingerly scoop the cooked dumplings out of the water with a slotted spoon, a few at a time, and arrange them on a large warm platter. Spoon the yogurt over the dumplings and the ground meat on top of that. Sprinkle with the dried mint and serve immediately.

WHAT THE COMMUNITY SAID

HOLLOWLEG: "This was amazing. And I added some of the leftover garlic yogurt to my scrambled eggs this morning. Some of the best scrambled eggs I've ever made!"

sam1148: "That's a wonderful recipe. I think it would make a great bento box lunch item, packing the sauce in the little compartments and the dumplings and meat in the main container for rewarming."

Morel Crostini

By Waverly / *Serves 4 to 6*

WHO: Waverly, formerly a lawyer, is now a mother living in Texas. She blogs at www.peaceandlove inthekitchen.com.

WHAT: A simple and versatile preparation for fresh morels.

HOW: Sauté the morels in butter with lemon juice, sliced leeks, and herbs, then use them to top homemade crostini along with some soft goat cheese.

WHY WE LOVE IT: When we announced this contest, we were hoping someone would submit a recipe that really embraced the rich, loamy quality of morels, rather than dousing them in cream or mixing them with other types of mushrooms, and this dish does just that.

Toasts

1 baguette, thinly sliced

Extra virgin olive oil

Topping

3 tablespoons unsalted butter

6 ounces fresh morels, cleaned and sliced
   lengthwise

2 teaspoons fresh thyme leaves

Salt and freshly ground black pepper

¾ cup thinly sliced leeks (white and
   pale green parts only)

1 teaspoon fresh lemon juice

2 tablespoons roughly chopped fresh
   flat-leaf parsley

Soft goat cheese

1. To make the toasts: Heat the oven to 350°F.

2. Arrange the sliced bread on a baking sheet and brush each slice with olive oil. Bake until the bread is lightly toasted, 10 to 15 minutes. Arrange the toasts on a serving tray.

3. In a large skillet, melt the butter over medium-high heat. Add the morels and sauté for 2 to 3 minutes, until they soften. Add the thyme, season with salt and pepper, and sauté until the morels are tender, about 3 minutes.

4. Add the leeks and sauté until soft, 3 to 4 minutes more. Stir in the lemon juice and parsley. Season to taste with salt and pepper.

5. Pour the mixture into a small serving bowl and put the bowl on the serving tray with the toasts. Put the goat cheese on the serving tray. Let everyone assemble their own crostini: Smear a bit of goat cheese on toast, then top with a spoonful of morels.

WHAT THE COMMUNITY SAID

WAVERLY: "You can use this delicious concoction many ways—in an omelet, over pasta, or as a side to beef."

BOULANGERE: "The bright spring flavors here are lovely."

OUI, CHEF: "Morels are precious, which is why if you are lucky enough to score some lovely fresh ones, you should put them to their highest and best use in a recipe like this one."

Late-Night Coffee-Brined Chicken

By gingerroot / *Serves 4*

WHO: Read more about gingerroot and see her recipe for Roasted Radish and Potato Salad with Black Mustard and Cumin Seeds on page 9; see her recipe for Chèvre Devils on page 62.

WHAT: We nicknamed this recipe Breakfast Chicken, since it includes the morning triumvirate: coffee, orange juice, and milk.

HOW: You brine a whole chicken in spiced coffee and orange juice, rub it with brown sugar and brown the skin, and then cook it in milk.

WHY WE LOVE IT: Like pork braised in milk, gingerroot's roast chicken emerges from the pot tender and melting, and it has a beautiful burnished exterior wherever the skin hasn't been submerged in the liquid. The smoky flavor is subtle but discernable—and unlike anything we can recall.

Brine

½ cup kosher salt

2 teaspoons black peppercorns

3 star anise

1 teaspoon whole cloves

2 juicy navel oranges, halved

2 cups hot strong coffee

3 cups ice cubes

Chicken

One 4- to 5-pound chicken, preferably organic

2½ tablespoons brown sugar

1½ tablespoons unsalted butter

2 cups 1% milk

1. To make the brine: Combine the salt, peppercorns, star anise, and cloves in a medium saucepan. Lightly crush the spices with the back of a large spoon. Squeeze the oranges over the spices, then add the orange halves themselves. Pour the coffee over the mixture, stir, and cover the pan. Allow the brine to steep for 10 minutes.

2. Meanwhile, pat the chicken dry. Place the chicken in a 2-gallon plastic bag.

3. Put the ice in a large bowl. Add the coffee brine and stir until the ice melts. Pour the brine (including the orange halves) into the bag with the chicken, seal the bag, and allow to sit at room temperature for 2 to 3 hours.

4. Remove the chicken from the brine, pat dry, and put in a large bowl. Let dry out for an hour in the refrigerator.

5. Heat the oven to 375°F.

6. Remove the chicken from the refrigerator and pat dry. Rub all over with the brown sugar.

7. Melt the butter in a Dutch oven or other heavy ovenproof pot over medium heat and brown the chicken well all over.

8. Add the milk, cover the pot, and transfer it to the oven. Cook for 1 hour, then remove the lid and continue to cook for another 20 to 40 minutes, or until the internal temperature of the chicken thigh registers 165°F.

9. Serve the chicken whole, or pull the meat off the bones and serve with wilted greens and rice. Be sure to spoon some of the cooking liquid over the meat.

WHAT THE COMMUNITY SAID

JONAHGAIL: "I've been dreaming about this recipe since you posted it, and the chicken defrosting in my fridge whispered the same thing to me: 'It's now or never.' So, despite the blistering heat wave, I turned on the oven and brined me a bird . . . and, *wow*, was it ever worth it! (And, as an added bonus, the stock made from the carcass was also amazing!)"

MOTHERWOULDKNOW: "With a shorter brining time than most brined-poultry recipes, it's doable for the folks like me who can't get it together to prepare a brine the night before."

Sunday Pork Ragu

By cookinginvictoria / Serves at least 4, with lots of leftover sauce

WHO: cookinginvictoria is an editor, writer, and mom who lives in Victoria, British Columbia.

WHAT: An old-school pork ragu that calls for actual bones.

HOW: Roast the pork bones with both hot and sweet sausage before bathing them in tomatoes and aromatics and then letting everything bubble gently for several hours.

WHY WE LOVE IT: It's uncomplicated, and nothing is done without good reason. It's a Sunday sauce worthy of passing on.

12 ounces meaty pork rib bones, cut into approximately 2-inch pieces (have your butcher cut them)

Salt

5 links sweet Italian sausage, casings removed

3 links spicy Italian sausage, casings removed

2 tablespoons extra virgin olive oil

1 medium yellow onion, cut into medium-small dice

6 small garlic cloves, coarsely chopped

One 5½-ounce can tomato paste

Two 28-ounce cans whole tomatoes

1 bay leaf

Freshly ground black pepper

½ cup chopped fresh flat-leaf parsley

1 pound dried pasta (rigatoni or penne rigate are best)

½ cup freshly grated Pecorino Romano cheese, plus more for serving

½ cup fresh basil leaves, cut into chiffonade

1. Heat the oven to 400°F.

2. Line a rimmed baking sheet with aluminum foil. Put a baking rack over the foil and arrange the bones on the rack. There should be a little space between them. Sprinkle with ½ teaspoon salt. Roast the bones for 30 to 40 minutes (you may have to turn any bigger pieces halfway through), until nicely browned and caramelized. Remove the pan from the oven and use tongs to transfer the ribs to a paper-towel-lined plate. Set the pan aside.

3. Slice each sausage link into 4 pieces (or simply pinch off chunks of sausage). Set the pieces of sausage on the rack (no need to wash it in between) and roast for about 30 minutes, or until browned and caramelized.

4. Heat a large Dutch oven over medium-low heat. Add the olive oil. When the oil has warmed, add the onion and sauté until just beginning to turn golden brown, about 10 minutes, stirring occasionally with a wooden spoon. Add the garlic and stir frequently until the aroma becomes heady and fragrant (watch carefully to make sure the garlic doesn't brown too quickly). Clear a spot in the pot with your wooden spoon, add the tomato paste (reserving the can) to the spot, and sauté for 1 to 2 minutes, just until it begins to release its fragrance. Mix the tomato paste into the onion and garlic mixture, then fill the tomato paste can with water and add it to the pot.

5. Drain the juice from the canned tomatoes and reserve about a cup of it. Add the bay leaf and the drained tomatoes to the pot: You can add the tomatoes whole—they will cook down; or simply cut each tomato into about 4 pieces with kitchen shears before adding them to the pot. Bring the mixture to a simmer and add the pork bones and sausages, nestling them carefully into the sauce. Lower the heat and cook at a low simmer for about 2 hours, stirring occasionally. During the first hour of cooking, if the sauce in the pan begins to reduce too much, add the reserved tomato liquid as needed. After the first hour of cooking, add water to the sauce instead if it's looking too thick. The sauce will smell wonderful as it cooks, infusing your home with pork and tomato aromas. Inhale and savor, and pour yourself a glass of your favorite red wine.

6. After about 2 hours of cooking, begin to add salt to the sauce, about 1 teaspoon at a time; let the sauce cook for about 15 minutes each time before tasting and adding more. Add a few grinds of black pepper and the parsley. Taste and adjust the seasonings until the flavors are to your liking. The total cooking time should be at least 2½ to 3 hours, but, honestly, you cannot cook this sauce too much. The longer it simmers, the better it will taste.

7. Meanwhile, about half an hour before you are ready to eat, fill a large pot with water. Bring to a boil and add a tablespoon or two of salt. Taste it and see if you can taste the salt—if you can't, add a little more. When the water is rapidly boiling, add the pasta. Give it a good stir with a slotted spoon and bring back to a boil. Cook for about 8 minutes, then begin tasting the pasta. When it is al dente, drain it, reserving a cup or two of the cooking water.

8. If the sauce looks too thick, add a ladleful or two of pasta water. Warm a big serving bowl with some of the pasta water, then drain it. Add a ladleful of sauce to the bowl. Top with a tablespoon or two of pecorino. Add a few large spoonfuls of pasta. Top with sauce, more cheese, and a sprinkling of basil. Add another layer of pasta, sauce, cheese, and basil. Keep layering the ingredients, then arrange the bones and sausage around the edges of the bowl. Top with a handful of basil and more cheese.

9. Serve the ragu with additional grated cheese and basil. Pour some red wine, and serve with warm bread. Enjoy!

WHAT THE COMMUNITY SAID

GINGERROOT: "I made this yesterday for Mother's Day dinner, and what a lovely way to spend the day! The aroma as the ragu bubbles away is amazing and definitely had everyone eager for dinner. Everyone was rewarded for their patience—it was so good!! I was able to source neck bones, and you're right: Enjoying them is a wonderful part of this recipe. Thank you again for sharing this. My family will enjoy this for years to come."

TIPS AND TECHNIQUES

A&M: You can pluck out the bones before serving, but we preferred to leave them in—just make sure to warn your eaters!

Sweet-and-Spicy Calamari

By SouffleBombay / *Serves 6*

WHO: SouffleBombay lives in Pennsylvania. She coauthored a cookbook for kids called *Picture Me Cooking.*

WHAT: A delicate version of fried calamari with a lively chile dipping sauce.

HOW: The calamari is simply tossed in flour, salt, black pepper, and cayenne before frying, allowing it to take center stage. The chile sauce is spiked with honey and sesame oil.

WHY WE LOVE IT: We liked SouffleBombay's technique of soaking the calamari rings in club soda before dredging them in the seasoned flour—it seemed to firm up the rings (in a pleasant way) before frying. The crisp coating is thin and delicate, swaddling the calamari like a silk scarf rather than a wooly muffler.

Calamari

¾ cup club soda

1 pound calamari tubes (frozen is fine),
   sliced into rings about ¼ inch wide

1 cup all-purpose flour

½ teaspoon cayenne pepper

3 dashes each salt and freshly ground black
   pepper

Vegetable oil for deep-frying

Sesame seeds for garnish (optional)

Sauce

¼ cup chile garlic sauce

6 tablespoons honey

½ teaspoon Asian sesame oil

1. Pour the club soda into a medium bowl, add the calamari rings, and stir until all are submerged. Let sit for 10 minutes.

2. Meanwhile, combine the flour, cayenne, salt, and pepper in another medium bowl and toss until combined. Set aside.

3. To make the sauce: In a small bowl, combine the chile garlic sauce, honey, and sesame oil. Mix well and set aside.

4. Drain the calamari and blot dry.

5. Heat 1 to 2 inches of oil to 375°F in a deep heavy pot. Dredge the rings in the flour mixture and set on a plate. Add one-quarter of the calamari to the hot oil and fry for 1½ to 2 minutes, or until golden; don't overcrowd the pot. Using a slotted spoon, lift out the calamari, put on a paper-towel-lined plate, and blot gently. Repeat.

6. Toss the calamari with the sauce and garnish with sesame seeds if you happen to have them on hand, or serve the sauce alongside the calamari. Enjoy!

WHAT THE COMMUNITY SAID

CHEFMOMMY: "I think this would be an excellent appetizer for someone who has never tried squid such as myself. I love the sweet-spicy combination as well as the delicate crunch of the calamari rings."

Shaved Asparagus and Mint Salad

By meatballs&milkshakes / *Serves 4*

WHO: meatballs&milkshakes lives in New York. She blogs at www.meatballsandmilkshakes .wordpress.com.

WHAT: A crisp, bright salad of shaved asparagus, Parmesan, mint, and hazelnuts.

HOW: Get out your keenest vegetable peeler. It does double duty here, first with the asparagus and then with the Parmesan cheese.

WHY WE LOVE IT: The pert, woodsy flavor of asparagus is sometimes lost once it's cooked—this salad preserves that flavor, and the long ribbons give each bite a wholesome crunch.

1 bunch asparagus, tough ends removed

A handful of roughly chopped toasted hazelnuts

1 tablespoon chopped fresh mint

3 tablespoons fresh lemon juice

2 tablespoons sherry vinegar

1 teaspoon honey

3 tablespoons extra virgin olive oil

Salt and freshly ground black pepper

A chunk of Parmesan or pecorino cheese for shaving

1. Using a vegetable peeler, shave the asparagus lengthwise into long strips. Toss in a bowl with the hazelnuts and mint.

2. In a small bowl, whisk together the lemon juice, vinegar, honey, and olive oil. Pour the dressing over the asparagus and toss gently, adding salt and pepper to taste. Shave some Parmesan on top and serve.

MEATBALLS&MILKSHAKES: "This also makes fantastic leftovers the next morning. Just put a little on top of a buttered, toasted piece of nice bread or brioche, and top with a poached or fried egg and a little more of the vinaigrette."

LMAYB6: "Love the idea of shaved asparagus for the foundation of a salad. It puts a whole new twist on salad greens!"

NANP: "This is my new favorite late-spring and summer meal. I add ribbons of summer squash to give some color contrast."

Sausage and Kale
Dinner Tart

By My Pantry Shelf / *Serves 6*

WHO: My Pantry Shelf is a science teacher living in Sonoma County, California. She blogs at www
.mypantryshelf.com.

WHAT: A lazy meal in its own right that makes for an instant dinner party—all that's needed is a big
green salad and plenty of wine.

HOW: A flaky pastry base and judicious amounts of ricotta, white wine, and fresh basil go a long
way in dressing up the rustic kale and sausage filling.

WHY WE LOVE IT: You can impress dinner guests without chipping away at your bank account: This
beauty coaxes luxury out of spare ingredients and bends readily to adaptation, depending on what
looks good at the market and what you have on hand.

Tart Shell

8 tablespoons (1 stick) chilled unsalted butter,
   cut into small cubes

1½ cups all-purpose flour, plus more for rolling

Pinch of salt

3 to 4 tablespoons ice water

Filling

1 tablespoon olive oil

1 tablespoon unsalted butter

2 cups minced onions

2 garlic cloves, minced

Salt and freshly ground black pepper

8 ounces sweet Italian sausage, casings
   removed

1 large bunch dinosaur (or cavalo nero) kale,
   stemmed and roughly chopped

¼ cup dry white wine

½ cup fresh basil leaves, slivered

1 large egg

¼ cup ricotta or other fresh cheese, such as feta
   or goat cheese

1. To make the tart shell: Combine the butter, flour, and salt in the bowl of a food processor. Pulse until the butter is in pea-sized pieces. While pulsing, slowly drizzle the ice water through the top feed tube into the food processor; you have added enough water when the dough sticks together when pressed.

2. Remove the dough and shape it gently into a disk. Wrap the disk in plastic and chill for at least 30 minutes.

3. Unwrap the dough and place it on a lightly floured board. Using a floured rolling pin, roll the dough into a circle about 12 inches in diameter. Press it gently into the bottom and up the sides of a 10-inch tart pan with a removable bottom. Prick the bottom of the crust all over with a fork. Lay a piece of parchment paper or foil over the dough and fill it with beans or pie weights. Refrigerate for at least 20 minutes.

4. Heat the oven to 400°F.

5. Bake the tart shell for 20 minutes, then remove the parchment and weights and bake for an additional 5 minutes, or until the crust no longer looks wet and has begun to brown. Set the tart shell on a rack to cool while you prepare the filling. Leave the oven on.

6. To make the filling: Heat the oil and butter in a large skillet over medium heat. Once the butter melts, add the onions and garlic, reduce the heat to medium-low, and cook until the onions are soft and light brown, 5 to 7 minutes. Season with salt and pepper. Remove the onions with a slotted spoon and place in a large bowl.

7. Increase the heat to medium and add the sausage. Brown it well, breaking it up into small pieces, about 5 minutes. Remove the sausage from the pan and put in the bowl with the onions. Drain all but 1 tablespoon of the fat from the pan.

8. Add the kale to the pan. Pour the wine over the kale, scrape up any bits from the bottom of the pan, and cover it. Cook for 3 to 5 minutes, until the kale is wilted. If the kale is still very wet, cook it uncovered for another minute or two, until it's quite dry. Season with salt and pepper.

9. Add the kale to the onions and sausage, toss everything together, and allow the mixture to cool for 5 minutes.

10. Add the basil, egg, and ricotta to the kale mixture and toss gently to combine. Season with salt and pepper. Spoon the mixture into the cooked tart shell, making sure to cover the bottom evenly.

11. Put the tart on a baking sheet and bake for 10 to 15 minutes, until the filling is set and the tart shell is nicely brown. Cool the tart for a few minutes on a wire rack, then slice and serve.

WHAT THE COMMUNITY SAID

DABBLINGS: "I made this tonight for dinner using some homemade Italian sausage and some of the first kale of the season from our garden. My two-year-old son liked it so much he put down his dessert and asked for more. Thanks for sharing!"

MARIARAYNAL: "I made this yesterday, and it was wonderful. Just wonderful. It would be excellent at brunch as well, and I also think the filling would be terrific over pasta."

SUMMER

Shrimp Burgers with Roasted Garlic–Orange Aioli

By EmilyC / *Serves 4*

WHO: EmilyC, a home cook, lives in Arlington, Virginia.

WHAT: Fennel-and-orange-infused shrimp burgers on brioche buns slicked with aioli.

HOW: Can be sautéed in a skillet or grilled.

WHY WE LOVE IT: EmilyC caramelizes the fennel for the burgers. For the aioli, she forgoes the wallop of raw garlic and the more common lemon for the mellow, floral flavors of roasted garlic and orange, and she cleverly uses the aioli not once but twice: to bind the shrimp patties (we used 2 teaspoons, but you may want more) and to spread on the buns.

5 tablespoons extra virgin olive oil

¼ cup finely chopped fennel bulb, plus 2 tablespoons finely chopped fennel fronds

¼ cup finely chopped shallots

¼ cup finely chopped red bell pepper

1 tablespoon finely chopped fresh chives

1 tablespoon grated orange zest

1½ pounds shrimp, peeled, deveined, and finely chopped (by hand)

Kosher salt and freshly ground black pepper

1 to 2 tablespoons Roasted Garlic–Orange Aioli (recipe follows)

4 hamburger or other buns (brioche is nice), toasted

1. In a large sauté pan, heat 2 tablespoons of the olive oil over medium heat. Add the chopped fennel bulb and shallots and cook until they start to caramelize, about 8 minutes. Add the red pepper and cook for about 3 minutes; you want the pepper to soften but retain some texture. Remove from the heat and mix in the fennel fronds, chives, and orange zest.

2. In a large bowl, combine the shrimp with the sautéed vegetable mixture and salt and pepper to taste. Fold in enough aioli, a teaspoon at a time, just to bind the burgers. Form into 4 patties and refrigerate until ready to cook.

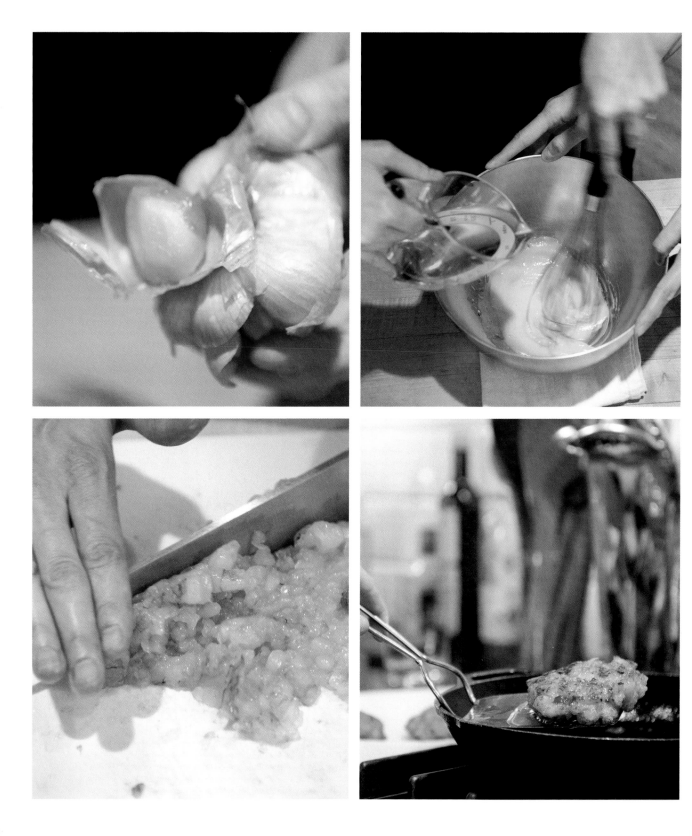

3. Heat the remaining 3 tablespoons olive oil in a large frying pan (cast iron works well) over medium-high heat. Fry the patties until golden and cooked through, about 4 minutes on each side.

4. Spread aioli on both sides of the toasted buns, and assemble the burgers, using your favorite accompaniments, such as big leaves of buttercrunch lettuce.

Roasted Garlic–Orange Aioli

1 head of garlic	Kosher salt
½ cup plus 1 tablespoon extra virgin olive oil	2 tablespoons fresh orange juice
2 large egg yolks, at room temperature	1 teaspoon finely grated orange zest
½ cup grapeseed or vegetable oil	Freshly ground black pepper

1. Heat the oven to 400°F. Peel away the outer skin of the garlic head and cut off the top ¼ to ½ inch to expose the individual cloves. Drizzle 1 tablespoon of the olive oil over the garlic, wrap it in foil, and roast for 30 to 35 minutes, until the cloves are soft when pressed. Let cool.

2. Squeeze the garlic cloves from their skin. Mash 3 cloves and set aside, reserving the rest for another use.

3. In a medium bowl, whisk the egg yolks. Gradually whisk in the remaining ½ cup olive oil, then the grapeseed oil—begin with small drizzles, then whisk in a thin stream until the mayo is very thick. Whisk in a pinch of salt, then the orange juice a little at a time (you may not need the full amount). Whisk in the orange zest and the roasted garlic paste. Season with salt and pepper.

WHAT THE COMMUNITY SAID

BOULANGERE: "Huge success! Like throwing fish to seals. I added 2 eggs to help bind them."
RHONDA35: "I think they'd be great on little buns as shrimp sliders for an hors d'oeuvre."

TIPS AND TECHNIQUES

A&M: For the aioli's flavors to fully develop, we recommend making it the day before and letting it hang out in the fridge overnight, tightly covered. And to make sure the burgers stick together, make sure you chop the shrimp very fine.

A Tribute to Woody
(Homemade Ginger Ale Float)

By inpatskitchen / *Serves 2*

WHO: inpatskitchen is a retired teacher, paralegal, and seafood retailer. She lives in Troy, Michigan, and blogs at www.inpatskitchen.blogspot.com.

WHAT: A homemade version of Vernor's Ginger Ale from Michigan, used to make a classic float (or shake).

HOW: For the ginger ale, fresh ginger, vanilla, and light brown sugar are cooked down to an intense syrup.

WHY WE LOVE IT: With not much work, you get a kicky homemade ginger syrup; combined with seltzer, it's a fitting ode to a proud Michigan soda pop tradition. The syrup is made with a handful of ingredients you probably have socked away in your kitchen—your hot, sticky kitchen: best go make yourself a float.

6 large scoops great-quality vanilla ice cream

½ cup Ginger Syrup (recipe follows)

3 cups seltzer

1. For a shake: Place the ice cream, syrup, and seltzer in a blender and blend until smooth. Pour into 2 tall glasses and grab some straws.

2. For a float: Place 3 scoops of ice cream in each of 2 tall glasses. Mix the syrup with the seltzer and then pour half into each ice-cream-filled glass. Grab the straws and 2 long spoons!

Ginger Syrup

½ cup thinly sliced fresh ginger

½ cup granulated sugar

¼ cup packed light brown sugar

¼ teaspoon vanilla extract

i. Combine the ginger, both sugars, and 1½ cups water in a saucepan and bring to a boil. Simmer for about 15 minutes, or until liquid is reduced to 1 cup. Remove from the heat, stir in the vanilla, and let cool; strain.

WHAT THE COMMUNITY SAID

SUE D: "Tried this recipe about a month ago and have been dreaming of making more ever since. This wonderful recipe is simple, refreshing, and fantastically bright-tasting. I can never again sip commercially made ginger ale—this recipe ended that practice. My experience of making and enjoying this amazing beverage was a satisfying adventure!"

LIZTHECHEF: "Congratulations! We drank Vernor's when I was a student at Kalamazoo College—great for hangovers. Love your recipe!"

SFMILLER: "Fun recipe that evoked major food memories. Growing up in central Michigan, I put away dozens of Vernor's floats as a kid. What we called a Boston Cooler was Vernor's and vanilla ice cream blended like a milk shake—which is darn good too."

Okonomiyaki

By Midge / *Makes roughly 12 pancakes*

WHO: Read more about Midge and see her recipe for Burnt Caramel Pudding on page 155; see her recipe for Grown-Up Birthday Cake on page 186.

WHAT: Eggy and crisp Kyoto-style pancakes are studded with plump morsels of tender shrimp and threaded through with ribbons of cabbage and rings of scallion.

HOW: If you can make pancakes, you can make okonomiyaki.

WHY WE LOVE IT: The savory batter is enriched with a dash of sesame oil and soy sauce, and the accompanying soy-and-Sriracha mayo is a zippy accent. We tore off bite-size pieces of pancake and dunked them in the sauce before gobbling them down.

Sauce

½ cup mayonnaise

2 tablespoons soy sauce

2 teaspoons Sriracha, or to taste

Pancakes

5 large eggs

1 teaspoon soy sauce

1 teaspoon sesame oil

1 teaspoon sea salt

⅓ cup all-purpose flour

2 cups finely shredded cabbage

1 bunch scallions, trimmed and chopped

¾ cup raw baby shrimp or chopped larger shrimp

Canola oil for frying

1 to 2 tablespoons sesame seeds, toasted

Bonito flakes (optional)

1. To make the sauce: Whisk the ingredients together and voilà, your sauce. Set aside.

2. To make the pancakes: Heat the oven to 200°F.

3. In a large bowl, whisk the eggs with the soy sauce, sesame oil, and sea salt. Gradually add the flour, whisking until incorporated. Fold in the cabbage, scallions, and shrimp.

4. Warm a couple of glugs of canola oil in a large skillet (you want a thin film of oil) over medium-high heat until glistening. Ladle the batter into the skillet as you would for regular pancakes; I usually make them about the size of a saucer. Cook for about 3 minutes on each side, or until golden brown. Keep covered in the oven while you make the rest.

5. Scatter the sesame seeds and/or bonito flakes on top of the pancakes and serve with the dipping sauce and a cold pilsner.

WHAT THE COMMUNITY SAID

BABS1652: "We dream about these morsels of marvelousness. Seriously! My family would eat these every day if I made them. We have had them with shrimp and with chicken and with three kinds of cabbage. The only change I made was to use sambal (Indonesian hot sauce) instead of the Sriracha, because that is what I had in the house."

GINGERROOT: "I used brown rice flour to accommodate my gluten-free husband and the pancakes were perfect. I also threw in some cilantro and shiso."

TIPS AND TECHNIQUES

RYANBISSOON: "Don't make the batter too far in advance, as the cabbage will leach a lot of water, making the batter too wet."

Salvadoran Breakfast Pancakes (aka Quesadillas)

By Sasha (Global Table Adventure) / *Makes 18 quesadillas*

WHO: Sasha is a mom and food writer living in Tulsa, Oklahoma. She blogs at www.globaltablead
venture.com.

WHAT: Salvadoran "quesadillas" with a unique blend of sweet, savory, and tangy flavors and the
texture of a fine, delicate corn muffin.

HOW: Mix the batter in just a few minutes and spoon it into muffin tins.

WHY WE LOVE IT: We were instantly won over by these mysterious, ethereal breakfast cakes. Even
the uncooked batter, a cloud of sugar, butter, sour cream, and rice flour lightened with egg and perfumed with Parmesan, inspired rhapsodic musings. The edges of the little cakes crisp and brown
beautifully, while the centers remain snow white and tender.

1 cup rice flour

1 teaspoon baking powder

Pinch of salt

½ pound (2 sticks) unsalted butter, at room
   temperature

1 cup sugar

3 large eggs

1 cup sour cream

½ cup grated hard cheese such as cotija or
   Parmesan

Sesame seeds for sprinkling

1. Heat the oven to 350°F. Grease 18 muffin cups.

2. Whisk together the rice flour, baking powder, and salt.

3. In the bowl of a stand mixer fitted with the paddle attachment, cream the butter with the sugar.
    Add the eggs one at a time, mixing until fully incorporated. Scrape down the sides as needed.
    Beat in the sour cream, cheese, and rice flour mixture until a smooth batter forms.

4. Spoon into the greased muffin tins, filling each one four-fifths of the way (this batter does not
    rise much). Sprinkle on sesame seeds to taste.

5. Bake until nut brown, 15 to 20 minutes. Let cool to room temperature. They taste like a cheesy pound cake; amazing with a cup of coffee in the morning.

WHAT THE COMMUNITY SAID

BORNTOBEWORN: "Made these this morning while at the beach on vacation. They are restaurant-worthy! I forgot to get sesame seeds, so we put some slivered almonds on top."

SEXYLAMBCHOPX: "I just popped these out of the pan. So rich and moist. I used a mini-muffin pan and it worked out great; exactly enough batter to make 24 mini-muffins."

TIPS AND TECHNIQUES

A&M: We recommend letting the cakes cool for at least 10 minutes before removing them from the pan—we found they slipped out easily this way.

Haricots Verts à la Dijonnaise

By AntoniaJames / *Serves 4*

WHO: Read more about AntoniaJames and see her recipe for Crispy Spice-Brined Pecans on page 120.

WHAT: The ultimate clean, crisp salad for a picnic (no wilting here), with summer's best produce—perky haricots verts, sweet cherry tomatoes, and crunchy Persian cucumber—accented by measured doses of anise, honey, and tarragon.

HOW: The dressing is enriched with a hard-boiled egg yolk and roasted garlic, two festive ingredients that make it special but still safe for a sunny day.

WHY WE LOVE IT: As aargersi, who first tested this recipe as a Community Pick, put it: "AntoniaJames is a master at layering flavors so that everything sings together and there is no one, pushy soloist."

1 tablespoon minced shallot

1 tablespoon tarragon vinegar

2 small Persian or 1 English cucumber, preferably organic

Kosher salt

Yolk of 1 hard-boiled egg

1 teaspoon honey, or more to taste, warmed

½ teaspoon grated lemon zest, or more to taste

1 tablespoon fresh lemon juice

1 teaspoon Dijon mustard

½ teaspoon anise seeds

2 medium roasted garlic cloves (see page 223 for instructions to roast garlic)

Sea salt

1 tablespoon extra virgin olive oil

1 pound haricots verts (some call them French beans) or green beans

12 to 14 cherry tomatoes, halved

Freshly ground black or white pepper

2 tablespoons finely chopped fresh flat-leaf parsley

1. In a very small dish, combine the shallot and vinegar; set aside.

2. Finely dice the cucumbers (leave the skin on if they are organic, peel them if not). Put them in the bowl in which you plan to make the salad. Sprinkle with salt and set aside.

3. In a small bowl, mash the hard-boiled egg yolk with the back of a small fork. Add the honey, lemon zest, lemon juice, and mustard and beat well to get rid of any lumps of yolk.

4. In a heavy mortar, crush the anise seeds with the roasted garlic and a pinch of salt and grind to a smooth paste. Add to the egg yolk and lemon mixture, then add the olive oil and whisk to combine.

5. Trim the beans and steam or blanch them to the degree of tenderness you like best. Plunge them into a basin of ice water when they're done to prevent further cooking. Drain and shake off any excess water.

6. Drain the water that has accumulated from the bowl of cucumbers. Add the cherry tomatoes and beans.

7. Drain the vinegar from the shallots into the bowl with the dressing. Mix well and add to the salad, along with the shallots. Gently toss. Taste for salt and add more if necessary. Add pepper to taste. Sprinkle on the parsley. Enjoy!

WHAT THE COMMUNITY SAID

SDEBRANGO: "I just finished making this salad for maybe the fifth or sixth time, and I remembered that I never told you how wonderful it is. I love the vinaigrette and use it on other salads as well. Just had it with steak and it's just so delicious."

CHEZSUZANNE: "The only change I might make next time is to toss the beans in the dressing while they're still warm to allow them to soak up the wonderfulness of the dressing. I can see this with some farro or barley too, for a great vegetarian entree. Really a wonderful recipe, AJ!"

TIPS AND TECHNIQUES

ANTONIAJAMES: "If taking this on a picnic, or making it ahead for a potluck, block party, etc., remember that the acids in the dressing and the cherry tomatoes will discolor the green beans if added too far in advance. So, instead of adding the tomatoes with the cucumbers and beans and then tossing with the dressing, drop the cut tomatoes into a medium jar with the dressing. Put the shallots and vinegar in that jar too, instead of on the salad. In essence, you combine the cucumbers and green beans in one container, and just before you're ready to serve, toss with the dressing, cherry tomatoes, and shallots."

Dilled Crunchy Sweet Corn Salad with Buttermilk Dressing

By creamtea / *Serves 6*

WHO: creamtea lives in New York City.

WHAT: A thoughtfully composed corn salad with a tart accomplice, buttermilk dressing.

HOW: No cooking! Just chopping and stirring.

WHY WE LOVE IT: The dressing, tangy with buttermilk and yogurt, envelops the crunchy corn, peppers, and cucumbers in a silky cloak. We love the hit of herbs (dill and parsley) and the zip of onion and garlic.

Salad

1 small shallot, halved lengthwise and thinly sliced

Salt

3 ears sweet corn, husked, kernels scraped from the cobs with a sharp knife (about 2¾ cups)

4 Persian or 1 English cucumber, quartered lengthwise and sliced crosswise into ½-inch-wide pieces

1 long red sweet pepper, cored, seeded, and diced

A small handful of dill (about 4 smallish sprigs), minced

¼ cup minced fresh flat-leaf parsley

Crumbled feta cheese, rinsed and drained, for garnish

Dressing

¼ cup buttermilk

⅔ cup yogurt (not Greek-style), stirred

1 tablespoon white wine vinegar

3 tablespoons minced Vidalia or other sweet onion

1 small garlic clove, minced and mashed with a pinch of salt

¼ cup extra virgin olive oil

Salt and freshly ground black pepper

1. To make the salad: Toss the shallot slices with ½ teaspoon salt and allow to sit for about 20 minutes to draw out any harshness. Rinse well and pat dry with a paper towel.

2. In a large bowl, toss the corn kernels lightly to separate them, then add the shallot and the remaining salad ingredients (except for the feta) and toss again to combine.

3. To make the dressing: In a small bowl, combine the buttermilk, yogurt, vinegar, onion, and garlic and whisk together. Add the oil in a slow stream, whisking until incorporated. Season with salt and pepper to taste. Refrigerate until slightly chilled.

4. Serve the salad, garnished with the feta cheese. Pass the dressing separately.

WHAT THE COMMUNITY SAID

MIDGE: "Made this for tonight and loved it. This, vinho verde, and ice cream are the perfect dinner when it's 102 degrees."

BLUEJEANGOURMET: "This was perfect last night with pulled pork and ribs! I added some of our backyard tomatoes to the salad, and it was fantastic."

SYLVIA9000: "This was mad tasty. Loved every kernel of it."

SAGEGREEN: "I used a thick Mideastern yogurt, which worked very well. The salad is pretty darn good without any dressing too!"

Raspberry Custard Cups

By SLD / *Serves 6*

WHO: SLD is an investigator who lives in Michigan.

WHAT: The brilliant love child of raspberry cheesecake and crème brûlée.

HOW: You fold tangy cream cheese into an egg-and-flour-enriched custard, which is then studded with plump whole raspberries and covered in a cap of rich brown sugar.

WHY WE LOVE IT: These are so easy you can make them with children. You can eat them with children, or you can serve them to adults and all feel like big, happy children.

⅓ cup sugar

1 large egg

1 tablespoon all-purpose flour

2 teaspoons cornstarch

1 cup whole milk

½ teaspoon vanilla extract

4 ounces cream cheese, cut into small pieces, at room temperature

2 cups fresh raspberries

¼ cup lightly packed light brown sugar

1. In a medium saucepan, combine the sugar, egg, flour, and cornstarch. Mix well. Add the milk and vanilla, whisking well. Bring to a boil over medium heat, whisking constantly. Cook, whisking, for 5 to 7 minutes, or until the custard thickens.

2. Pour the custard into a bowl, add the cream cheese, and whisk for 2 minutes, or until the cheese melts. Cover and refrigerate for at least 30 minutes, or until cool.

3. Heat the broiler. Pour the custard into 6 custard cups set on a baking sheet. Press the berries into the custard. Broil 4 inches from the heat for 2 minutes, or until the custard is golden in color.

4. Sprinkle with the brown sugar and set aside for 1 to 2 minutes, or until the sugar melts. Alternatively, if you want to brûlée the sugar, put them back under the broiler briefly. Be sure to watch them carefully, and pull them out when the sugar is bubbly but before it burns.

HARDLIKEARMOUR: "These look awesome, and anything that's the love child of cheesecake and crème brûlée has got to be delicious."

CONSTANTERRATIC: "After two months, I have to admit that I have made these custard cups three more times (I'm shameless). I omitted the cream cheese and overloaded the cooled custard with pomegranate arils, and I've found my go-to dessert for life, haha. Thank you again for a recipe that is so versatile and satisfying!"

FAVABEAN: "I added the juice of half a lemon, and the tartness tempered the sweetness. I also added a pinch or so of cardamom to the mixture, which was lovely."

TIPS AND TECHNIQUES

A&M: Because both options are already listed in SLD's recipe, you can simply brûlée the custard and then sprinkle the sugar on top, but we found that popping the ramekins back into the oven for a few minutes gave us that crisp shell we craved. The choice is yours—they're silky and delicious either way.

Boozy Watermelon Rosemary Lemonade

By piccantedolce / *Serves 6*

WHO: piccantedolce lives in Toronto; she blogs at www.piccantedolce.blogspot.com.

WHAT: A tart pink cocktail that is a burst of summer in a glass.

HOW: Puree watermelon with a rosemary syrup, then add booze.

WHY WE LOVE IT: You don't strain the watermelon puree, which gives the drink some texture. And we like that piccantedolce calls for gin instead of a more predictable spirit like vodka. We recommend you serve this in Mason jars over plenty of ice.

¾ cup sugar

4 fresh rosemary sprigs, plus 6 small
   sprigs for garnish

1 cup fresh lemon juice

7 cups watermelon cut into 1-inch (seedless)
   cubes (about ½ medium watermelon)

8 ounces gin

1 lemon, thinly sliced, for garnish

1. Place the sugar and 1 cup water in a small saucepan, add the 4 rosemary sprigs, and cook over medium heat, stirring, until the sugar dissolves. Remove from the heat, cover the saucepan, and let the syrup sit for at least 1 hour to infuse.

2. Put the lemon juice in a blender. Add the watermelon in batches, blending well. Pour in the rosemary simple syrup ¼ cup at a time until the mixture is at your desired sweetness (I use about 1 cup).

3. Pour the mixture into a large pitcher and add 1 cup cold water and the gin. Stir to combine. Serve over ice in jars or glasses, garnished with lemon slices and small rosemary sprigs.

WHAT THE COMMUNITY SAID

BOULANGERE: "The rosemary and gin are a brilliant combination. And I love that you're generous with the lemon. What a beautiful creation."

Flank Steak on Texas Toast with Chimichurri

By sdebrango / *Serves 4*

WHO: sdebrango lives in Brooklyn, New York.

WHAT: A sandwich that is a real two-hander, juicy and garlicky and fragrant.

HOW: You make one big batch of chimichurri, which both marinates the steak and gets swirled in to flavor the quickie aioli.

WHY WE LOVE IT: This steak prep technique—marinate, then dry-brine—made for one of the best steaks we've had lately, and the resulting sandwich shines because of it (the ripe tomatoes, buttery Texas toast, and aioli help, too).

Chimichurri

1 cup flat-leaf parsley leaves, finely chopped

½ cup baby arugula, finely chopped

2 garlic cloves, minced

¼ teaspoon dried oregano

¼ teaspoon red pepper flakes

½ cup plus 2 tablespoons extra virgin olive oil

2 tablespoons red wine vinegar

Salt and freshly ground black pepper to taste

Steak and Sandwich

One 1½- to 2-pound flank steak

Salt

1 ripe beefsteak or heirloom tomato

1 brioche Pullman loaf (or, if you prefer, a white Pullman loaf)

¼ cup mayonnaise

Freshly ground black pepper

Softened butter for the bread

1. To make the chimichurri: Place all the ingredients in a bowl and stir to combine.

2. Put the steak in a zip-top plastic bag, add half the chimichurri, seal the bag, and turn and tilt the bag to coat the steak on both sides. Refrigerate for 1 to 2 hours. Cover the rest of the chimichurri and refrigerate.

3. Approximately 45 minutes before you're planning to cook it, remove the steak from the refrigerator. Scrape off some of the chimichurri, salt the steak, and let it rest.

4. While the steak is resting, prepare the other ingredients: Slice the tomato. Cut the bread into ¾-inch-thick slices. Mix the mayonnaise and the reserved chimichurri together in a bowl.

5. When ready to sear the steak, pat it with a paper towel to remove excess moisture. Heat a large heavy skillet over medium-high heat until very hot. Lay the steak in the pan and let it sear without disturbing it. For medium-rare, cook for 3 to 4 minutes on each side. (You may have to adjust the time based on the thickness of the steak.) Remove from the pan, lay on a cutting board, season with pepper, and let rest for 5 to 10 minutes.

6. While the steak is resting, set a large heavy skillet over medium-high heat (if you have one with ridges, it will make nice grill marks on the bread). Spread butter on both sides of the bread, place in the hot pan, and cook for about one minute per side, until well toasted.

7. When the steak has rested, thinly slice it, cutting across the grain. To put your sandwiches together, spread chimichurri mayonnaise on one side of each slice of bread. Lay the sliced steak on half the slices of bread, add the tomato, put the other slices of bread on top, and enjoy.

WHAT THE COMMUNITY SAID

TEXAS EX: "Absolutely delicious. The bright flavors work perfectly together, and the sandwiches are a snap to prepare. Great recipe!"

BIGBEAR: "As good as anything I tasted in the corner *parillas* in the Belgrano District of Buenos Aires. That says a lot. Great sandwich, well deserving of the win."

ZOEMETROUK: "sdebrango, we made the steak on the grill this weekend with Jose Andrés' wrinkled potatoes. The steak was divine—the chimichurri took it to new heights."

TIPS AND TECHNIQUES

A&M: In divvying up the chimichurri, we scooped out mostly garlic and herbs to add to the mayo and held back on the oil so it didn't get too runny, and we were very happy. Very.

Braised Pork Belly Tacos with Watermelon, Jicama, and Jalapeño Salsa

By a la Alison / *Serves 3 to 4*

WHO: a la Alison lives in Philadelphia and works in advertising. She blogs at www.alaalison.com.

WHAT: Braised pork belly takes to warm, sweet allspice broth like a moth to a flame, and zippy watermelon, jicama, and jalapeño salsa is the perfect cool complement.

HOW: You'll want to plan ahead for the long brine and braise times, but the hands-on time is surprisingly minimal.

WHY WE LOVE IT: The pork emerges from the braising liquid burnished and melting, both spicy and a little sweet (there is minced chile in the braise as well). The crunchy salsa builds on the heat (and the sweet) and provides a great textural contrast. And there's nothing wrong with forgoing the tortillas, as we started to do at one point—just spoon some of the salsa over the pork belly and dig in.

Tacos

2 pounds pork belly

¾ cup honey

6 bay leaves

½ cup kosher or sea salt

2 tablespoons black peppercorns

3 tablespoons ground allspice

Salt and freshly ground black pepper

1 large shallot, minced

2 garlic cloves, minced

2 tablespoons minced seeded jalapeño

2 cups orange juice

1 cup chicken stock or low-sodium broth

10 to 12 small corn tortillas, warmed for serving

Salsa

3 cups cubed seedless watermelon

Juice of 1½ limes

1 cup diced peeled jicama

¼ cup chopped fresh cilantro

2 tablespoons minced seeded jalapeño

½ large red onion, minced

Salt

1. Rinse the pork and pat it dry.

2. To make the brine: Add 5 cups water, the honey, bay leaves, salt, and peppercorns to a small pot and bring to a boil. Remove the brine from the heat and allow to cool completely.

3. Place the pork in a large bowl and add the brine. Refrigerate for 6 to 7 hours (any more, and the pork will become too salty).

4. Remove the pork from the brine and pat completely dry. Allow to sit at room temperature for 30 minutes before braising. Heat the oven to 325°F.

5. Cut the pork belly into strips roughly 1 inch wide (about 10 strips). Season the strips with the allspice, salt, and pepper.

6. Heat a Dutch oven or other large ovenproof pot over medium heat. Once the pot is hot, add the strips fat side down and thoroughly brown the belly, 10 to 15 minutes. Flip and sear the other side for under a minute. Remove the pork to a paper-towel-lined plate.

7. Pour off most of the fat from the pot, leaving roughly 2 tablespoons. Add the shallot, garlic, and jalapeño to the Dutch oven and sauté in the pork fat for 5 minutes.

8. Return the pork to the pot and add the juice and stock. Bring to a slight simmer, place the lid on the pot, and move to the oven. Braise until the pork is very tender when pierced with a fork; this will take 2 to 3 hours.

9. Meanwhile, make the salsa: Mix all the ingredients together in a bowl and let stand while the pork cooks. This will allow the flavors to mix thoroughly before serving.

10. Remove the pork belly from the oven. To serve, top each warm tortilla with a strip of pork belly and a spoonful of salsa.

WHAT THE COMMUNITY SAID

MASTER CHEF SASS: "I consider myself to be somewhat of a pork belly enthusiast. And you, ma'am, sure know how to braise yourself a pork belly."

Corn Salad with Cilantro and Caramelized Onions

By Ms. T / *Serves 6*

WHO: Ms. T is a museum-marketing professional in Mill Valley, California. You can read about her cooking on her blog, www.stillsimmering.wordpress.com.

WHAT: Fresh corn meets sweet-and-sour onions.

HOW: Ms. T's version of this salad includes a technique we've never seen before: First she has you cook down red onion in balsamic vinegar and olive oil—and as the onion pieces soften into silky, purple jewels, they simultaneously create a rich, deeply flavored dressing for the salad.

WHY WE LOVE IT: Once you toss the luscious onion mass with crisp pancetta cubes, fresh cilantro, and barely cooked kernels of corn, you've got a corn salad that breaks new ground. We couldn't stop eating it, right from the bowl.

---

6 ears sweet corn, husked

Six ⅛-inch-thick slices pancetta, diced

¼ cup olive oil, or as needed

1 large red onion, chopped

2 tablespoons balsamic vinegar

2 teaspoons sugar

Salt

¼ cup finely chopped fresh cilantro

Freshly ground black pepper

---

1. Blanch the corn in a large pot of boiling water for about 3 minutes. Drain the corn and plunge it into a bowl of ice water to stop the cooking, then drain again and let cool completely.

2. Spread the pancetta in a large heavy skillet, set over medium heat, and cook until brown and crisp. Use a slotted spoon to transfer the pancetta to a plate lined with a paper towel.

3. Pour off most of the fat from the skillet, leaving a little goodness (pork fat) in the pan for cooking your onions. Add the oil, onions, vinegar, sugar, and a dash of salt to the pan and cook over

medium-low heat for 20 to 25 minutes, stirring frequently, until the onions are caramelized and most of the liquid has evaporated. Remove the pan from the heat.

4. Cut the corn kernels off the cobs and place in a large bowl. Add the onion mixture and cilantro and stir to combine. Season with salt and pepper and, if it seems dry, add a little more olive oil. (If you're making this ahead of time, cover and put it in the fridge. Take the salad out about 30 minutes before serving to take the chill off.)

5. Stir in the crisp pancetta just before serving.

WHAT THE COMMUNITY SAID

ADORRAIN: "Are you kidding me??? This is amazing. Absolutely amazing. Thank you for this perfect August-in-the-Midwest recipe. I can't wait to bring this to a potluck and be the star."

TIPS AND TECHNIQUES

ANTONIAJAMES: "Fresh marjoram would be perfect in this if you don't want to use cilantro. It's corn's best friend, though many people don't realize it. Use just the tiniest amount at first, adding more to taste, especially if you're picking your marjoram leaves off of a plant that's been in full sunlight/heat all day; the flavor of raw marjoram can be intense, especially under those circumstances."

State Fair Cream Puffs

By hardlikearmour / *Serves 6*

WHO: Read more about hardlikearmour and see her Coconut Cajeta and Chocolate Fondue on page 149.

WHAT: Easy-to-make cream puffs with a more boozy than chocolaty filling. hardlikearmour adapted her cream puffs recipe from the Wisconsin Bakers Association and her bourbon whipped cream from Rose Levy Beranbaum.

HOW: hardlikearmour cleverly presses the food processor into service to cool down the dough and then incorporate the eggs.

WHY WE LOVE IT: Purists will insist on stirring by hand, but this technique proves the elbow-grease method simply isn't necessary. She also uses an extra egg white for her puffs, which makes for bigger puffs that don't end up too gooey inside.

Cream Puffs

¼ cup whole milk

6 tablespoons unsalted butter,
   cut into ½-inch cubes

Heaping ¼ teaspoon salt

1 cup all-purpose flour

4 large eggs, 1 separated

Confectioners' sugar for dusting

Bourbon-Chocolate Whipped Cream

1 cup heavy cream

2 tablespoons Dutch-processed cocoa powder

2 tablespoons plus 2 teaspoons sugar

1 tablespoon bourbon (I used Knob Creek)

1. To make the cream puffs: Heat the oven to 425°F with a rack in the lower third. Spray a baking sheet lightly with cooking spray (to anchor the paper), then line with parchment paper. (Alternatively, use a Silpat mat.)

2. Combine ¾ cup water, the milk, butter, and salt in a heavy 2-quart saucepan and bring to a boil over medium-low heat. (The butter should melt before it boils.)

3. Meanwhile, whisk the flour for about 30 seconds to aerate and break up any clumps. In a 2-cup liquid measure, combine 3 eggs and 1 egg white and mix to blend. In a small bowl, whisk together the remaining yolk and 2 tablespoons water (this will be your egg wash).

4. Once the water has just started to boil, remove the pan from the heat and dump all of the flour in at once. Stir the mixture with a heatproof spatula until the flour is mostly incorporated. Return to the heat and use the spatula to smear the mixture across the bottom of the pan continuously for 3 to 4 minutes. A thin film of flour should build up on the bottom of the pan.

5. Transfer the dough to the bowl of a food processor and process for 15 seconds to cool slightly. With the processor running, add the eggs through the feed tube in a steady stream over about 15 seconds. Stop the processor and scrape down the sides of the bowl. Process for an additional 30 to 40 seconds, until a smooth paste has formed.

6. Transfer the dough to a gallon plastic bag, seal the bag, and cut a ½- to ¾-inch-long opening in one corner. Pipe the dough into a 2½- to 2¾-inch rounds about 1 inch high onto the lined baking sheet, making sure to leave about 2 inches between puffs. Brush the puffs with the egg wash, using the pastry brush to smooth the tops of the puffs as well as coat the puffs. Take care not to get the egg wash onto the baking sheet, as it will burn.

7. Bake for 10 minutes, then reduce the heat to 375°F and bake for 17 to 20 minutes, until the puffs are a deep golden brown. Turn the oven off.

8. Use a paring knife to cut a slit in the side of each puff (where you plan on cutting them in half). Place the tray of puffs back in the oven and use a wooden spoon to crack the door open. Allow the puffs to dry in the oven for 1 hour.

9. Remove the puffs from the oven and cool completely on a rack. (The puffs can be stored in an airtight container at room temperature for a day or two—recrisp for 3 minutes in a 350°F oven before serving.)

10. To make the whipped cream: Combine the cream, cocoa, and sugar in a medium bowl and whisk to combine. Cover and refrigerate for at least 1 hour to allow the cocoa to dissolve.

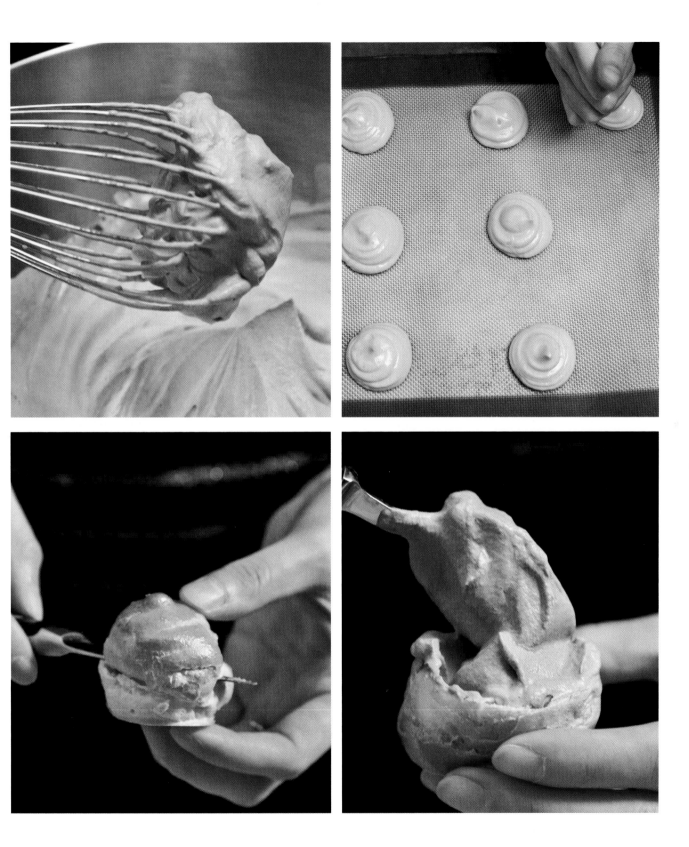

11. Whisk the cream by hand or beat with a hand mixer until stiff peaks form. Whisk in the bourbon.

12. To serve, cut the 6 prettiest cream puffs in half. Fill each with about ⅓ cup of the whipped cream, and dust with confectioners' sugar.

WHAT THE COMMUNITY SAID

H.C.R: "Gorgeous *and* more boozy than chocolaty? Perfect!"

BLUEKALEROAD: "This is a marvelous recipe. I'm using your bourbon chocolate whipped cream as a filling in a birthday cake."

TIPS AND TECHNIQUES

HARDLIKEARMOUR: "If you don't want to use bourbon, whisk in a teaspoon of vanilla extract instead to round out the chocolate flavor."

Baked Ricotta and Goat Cheese with Candied Tomatoes

By TheRunawaySpoon / *Serves 8 to 10*

WHO: Read more about TheRunawaySpoon and see her recipe for Fig and Blue Cheese Savouries on page 77; see her recipe for Pastitsio on page 105.

WHAT: A savory cheese cake topped with sweet tomato baubles.

HOW: Mix, drain, and bake your cheese. Blister your tomatoes in a hot pan and spoon them over.

WHY WE LOVE IT: The tomatoes really do taste like candy—the brown sugar and vermouth turn to syrup in the pan and cloak the cherry tomatoes, caramelizing their edges as they pop and start to collapse. Perch a slice of the creamy, salty ricotta and goat cheese cake on a piece of good baguette, then top it with a tomato and some syrup for the perfect bite.

One 15-ounce container whole milk ricotta

4 ounces fresh goat cheese

1 large egg

2 tablespoons fresh marjoram leaves (or other leafy herb of your choice), chopped if the leaves are large

Kosher salt and freshly ground black pepper

Baguette slices or crostini for serving

1 tablespoon olive oil

12 ounces cherry tomatoes

¼ cup sweet (Italian/red) vermouth

¼ cup packed light brown sugar

3 fresh marjoram sprigs (or other leafy herb of your choice)

Sea salt

1. To make the baked cheese: Place the ricotta in a colander lined with cheesecloth and leave to drain for about 30 minutes, gently pressing down with the back of a spoon or rubber spatula occasionally to help extract liquid.

2. Heat the oven to 375°F. Brush the inside of a 2-cup baking dish with olive oil.

3. In the bowl of a stand mixer fitted with the paddle attachment (or by hand with a wooden spoon in a large bowl), beat the ricotta, goat cheese, and egg until smooth. (Taste the goat cheese first—saltier cheeses will require less additional salt.) Beat in the herbs, salt to taste, and a generous amount of pepper.

4. Spoon the cheese mixture into the prepared baking dish. Bake for 40 minutes, or until puffed in the center and browning. Let the cheese cool slightly, then invert it onto a plate.

5. Meanwhile, make the tomatoes: Heat the olive oil in a large skillet over medium heat, then drop in the tomatoes. Cook, stirring frequently, until the skins start to split. Pull the pan off the flame and add the vermouth, then return to the heat. Add the brown sugar and herbs and stir until the sugar is melted. Add a generous pinch of sea salt. Lower the heat and cook gently until the liquid is reduced to a syrupy coating for the tomatoes. The tomatoes will collapse and some may disintegrate—that's fine, ideal even. You don't want them watery. Remove from the heat.

6. When ready to serve, spoon the candied tomatoes over the warm baked cheese and serve with sliced baguette or crostini.

WHAT THE COMMUNITY SAID

JAVA&FOAM: "Personally, I believe the tomatoes are the star of this dish. They are out of this world. Anyone who doesn't like tomatoes will be stunned at how incredible these taste. . . . Congrats on such an epic contribution to cocktail hour."

TIPS AND TECHNIQUES

THERUNAWAYSPOON: "The cheese mixture can be prepared a few hours in advance and then baked before serving. It is best served warm, but not right out of the oven. The tomatoes can be prepared ahead, too, and gently reheated before serving."

Peach Tart

By amanda / *Serves 8*

WHAT: Every cook needs a good dessert recipe that can be whipped up anywhere—this peach tart, with its easy press-in crust, is that recipe.

HOW: The dough, made with oil, milk, and almond extract, is pressed into the pan. There is no blind-baking nonsense. You just top the dough with the peaches, then shower them with a sugary, salty crumble and send the tart on its merry way into the oven.

WHY WE LOVE IT: It's sweet and salty, crisp yet gooey, and quite a looker too.

1½ cups plus 2 tablespoons all-purpose flour, or
    as needed

¾ teaspoon kosher salt

¾ cup plus 1 teaspoon sugar

¼ cup vegetable or canola oil

¼ cup mild olive oil

2 tablespoons whole milk

½ teaspoon almond extract

2 tablespoons cold unsalted butter

3 to 5 small ripe peaches, pitted and thickly
    sliced (about ½ inch wide)

1. Heat the oven to 425°F.

2. In a large bowl, stir together 1½ cups of the flour, ½ teaspoon of the salt, and the 1 teaspoon sugar. (Stirring enables the salt and sugar to "sift" the flour, so you don't need to sift it separately.)

3. In a small bowl, whisk together the oils, milk, and almond extract. Pour this mixture into the flour mixture and mix gently with a fork, just enough to dampen; do not overwork it. Transfer the dough to an 11-inch tart pan with a removable bottom (you can use a smaller one if necessary) and use your hands to pat the dough evenly over the bottom of the pan, pushing it up the sides to the edges. This will work if you pat firmly and confidently, not if you curl your fingertips into the dough. It should be about ⅛ inch thick all around; trim and discard excess dough.

4. In a medium bowl, combine the remaining ¾ cup sugar, 2 tablespoons flour, ¼ teaspoon salt, and the butter. (If your peaches are especially juicy, add 1 tablespoon additional flour.) Using your fingers, pinch the butter into the dry ingredients until crumbly, with a mixture of fine granules and tiny pebbles.

5. Starting at the outside, arrange the peaches in overlapping concentric circles over the dough; fill in the center in whatever pattern makes sense. The peaches should fit snugly. Sprinkle the pebbly butter mixture over the top (it will seem like a lot).

6. Bake for 35 to 45 minutes, until shiny, thick bubbles begin enveloping the fruit, and the crust is slightly brown. Cool on a rack, and serve warm or at room temperature, preferably with generous dollops of whipped cream.

WHAT THE COMMUNITY SAID

ROBIN O'D: "So good and easy! My twelve-year-old made most of the recipe, including pressing the crust into the pan. I love such a forgiving crust!"

FIVEANDSPICE: "This looks wonderful, Amanda! I love the shower of crumble over the top of the tart. A tart and a crisp all in one—what more could a person want?"

MYGARDENERSTABLE: "This is really a chameleon of a recipe, it is so incredibly versatile. I have made it countless times from Amanda's book over the years, not only with peaches. Today I made it with apples and 1 tablespoon of rum instead of almond extract, and it came out wonderfully."

TIPS AND TECHNIQUES

AMANDA: "I got the original recipe from my mother, who uses all vegetable oil in the crust. I use half vegetable oil and half olive oil. She neatly peels her peaches. Lazy kin, I do not. Hers is probably better, but you are stuck with mine."

CONTRIBUTORS

Alison Altomari,
a la Alison

Aliya LeeKong,
aliyaleekong

Amy Beadle Roth,
Minimally Invasive

Annaliese Bischoff,
Sagegreen

Arielle Arizpe,
arielleclementine

Ashley Jons,
wanderash

Barbara Reiss Newman,
drbabs

Carolyn Strashun,
Meatballs&Milkshakes

Catherine Gillespie,
singing_baker

Cathy Barrow,
MrsWheelbarrow

Christina DiLaura,
cdilaura

Christine Burns Rudalevige,
cheese1227

Colleen Kennedy,
SouffleBombay

Diana Chu,
monkeymom

Elizabeth Breuer,
OB Cookie

Elizabeth Van Huffel,
LocalSavour

Emily Connor,
EmilyC

Emily Nunn,
ENunn

Emily Vikre,
fiveandspice

Frances Ren Huang,
FrancesRenHuang

Helen Leah Conroy,
AntoniaJames

Hong and Kim Pham,
ravenouscouple

Jane Lyons,
cooklynveg

Jennifer Hess,
lastnightsdinner

Jennifer Hoffmeister,
piccantedolce

Jennifer Wagner,
SML Office

Jenny Engle,
gingerroot

Jessica Harper,
thecrabbycook

Julie Grice,
SavvyJulie

Karen Juul Wilkinson,
My Pantry Shelf

Katie Farmand,
TheThinChef

Katie Morford and Humaira Ghilzai

Katie Vitucci,
the parsley thief

Kelsey Yarnell,
amusebouche

Leslie Goldenberg,
sticksnscones

Lisanne Weinberg Lubitz,
creamtea

Liz Larkin,
mrslarkin

Lori Goldsby,
lorigoldsby

Lori Narlock,
lorinarlock

Lynda Balslev,
TasteFood

Margaret Loftus,
Midge

Meghan Kaminski,
MeghanVK

Melissa Villaveces,
melissav

Nonie Brzyski,
NWB

Pat Kallio,
inpatskitchen

Paul Joseph,
pauljoseph

Paula Marchese,
cookinginvictoria

Perre Coleman Magness,
TheRunawaySpoon

Rivka Friedman,
Rivka

Sara Grimes,
hardlikearmour

Sara Hafiz,
onetribegourmet

Sara Williamson,
Table9

Sherry Day,
SLD

Steven Dunn,
Oui, Chef

Susan Pridmore,
ChezSuzanne

Suzanne DeBrango,
sdebrango

Tiffany Zarem,
Ms. T

Waverly Gage,
Waverly

Will Reeve,
Reeve

Sasha Martin
Sasha (Global Table
Adventure)

Not Pictured:
Cnevertz
Cordelia

MENUS

FALL

Harvest Dinner

Mulled White Wine with Pear Brandy, 95

Roasted Carrot Soup, 165

Not-Too-Virtuous Salad with
Caramelized Apple Vinaigrette, 117

Warm Orzo Salad with Beets
and Greens, 80

Roasted Butterflied Chicken with
Cardamom and Yogurt, 175

Ginger Apple Torte, 51

Thanksgiving

Mulled White Wine with Pear Brandy, 95

Roasted Carrot Soup, 165

Caramelized Butternut Squash Wedges
with Sage Hazelnut Pesto, 36

Roasted Cauliflower with
Gremolata Bread Crumbs, 19

Vegetarian Mushroom Thyme Gravy, 43

Ginger Apple Torte, 51

One-Pot Meals

Pastitsio, 105

Hunter's-Style Chicken, 113

Moorish Paella, 30

Tamatar Biryani (Tomato Rice), 126

Weeknight Suppers

Lamb Merguez, 168

A Medley of Roasted Potatoes
with Homemade Za'atar and
Aleppo Pepper, 93

Linguine with Sardines, Fennel,
and Tomato, 129

Roasted Cauliflower with
Gremolata Bread Crumbs, 19

Roasted Carrot Soup, 165

Sausage and Kale Dinner Tart, 213

Warm Orzo Salad with Beets
and Greens, 80

Butternut Squash and Roasted Garlic
Galette, 55

ACKNOWLEDGMENTS

Since its inception, the sometimes chaotic, always hunger-inducing, and often soul-feeding universe that is Food52 has been slowly but surely expanding. We knew this to be true in a vague sort of way, as evidenced by the growing numbers of recipes submitted to our weekly contests and the fact that we always seemed to be in need of just one more chair at our offices in Manhattan. However, the reality of the growth that has taken place around us didn't fully sink in until it came time to write these acknowledgments. We thought of all the people who have been on board since early days, and of the newer faces as well—community members, staffers, and a very special, brand-new mini-Food52er (Clara Pauline, we're looking at you). They are the heartbeat of the wonderful place we call Food52, generously giving our hungry little child all of the love and late nights that it needs along the way. This book belongs to all of them.

In the year since the first cookbook was published, we have watched our online community swell to (at last count) 85,000 members strong. We've found new ways to engage, ways for our kitchens to get a little closer—which, of course, is at the core of everything that we do. From our first-ever iPad app to the birth of the Food52 Hotline, growing the site has been a tremendous undertaking, and we couldn't have done it without the help of all of the top-notch people we are honored to call a part of the Food52 family.

We knew early on that ours was a community of particularly talented home cooks. Saturating the site with their soulful, storied recipes, they breathed warmth and life into the burgeoning world we'd created for them. A few of these Food52ers have engaged with us on such a level that we want take this moment to thank them in particular.

It has been exciting to welcome one of our own deeper into the fold—Tom Hirschfeld, photojournalist and chef turned farmer, father, and now Food52 columnist, whose quietude and passionate engagement with food and cooking started seeping into the fabric of our site from the moment he joined. Cathy Barrow and Kim Foster hosted the meaty monthly challenges of Charcutepalooza with unparalleled gusto and shared it with us at Food52. Sharon Knoll has helped make the Food52 Hotline into an intelligent and remarkably spam-free place for cooking questions of all sorts by meticulously flagging anything that seems out of place. Sara Grimes has shepherded us through many a Community Picks dibs-calling, spreading the recipe-testing love with grace and easing our load simply because she can. A big thank-you to you all, and to countless others, for inspiring us to always be a little bit better and reminding us every day why home cooks are so very special.

Beautiful photographs define this book as they do our site, and we have a team of phenomenally talented photographers to thank for that: Sarah Shatz, James Ransom, Melanie Einzig, and Jennifer Causey brought life to the book. They tackle the particular challenge that food so often presents with artistry and heart, somehow managing to make even the most uncooperative of dishes (ahem, Broccoli Cooked Forever) look as delicious as they taste.

We have assembled the very best staff there is, a feat we would toast every single day given the opportunity. At the helm is Alexandra Lutz, our president, who pushes us to dream big and think in new ways, to look beyond our little corner of the internet, see a bigger world, and seek out our place in it. Kristen Miglore, our "Genius" Senior Editor, has a gentle presence and easy humor that keeps us at once on track and giggling each and every day. Her value is immeasurable. Head Recipe Tester Stephanie Bourgeois and Test Kitchen Manager Jennifer Vogliano run the recipe-testing show, whipping up perfectly executed, photo-ready recipes without batting an eye. Supporting them and cooking up a storm for us in each of their respective kitchens is a whole team of behind-the-scenes recipe testers: Victoria Ross, Natalie Barbarese, Annie Petito, Marisa Robertson-Textor, Rebecca Marx, Nora Singley, Andrea Lynn, Lauren Utvich, Pervaiz Shallwani, Paul Darrah, Rebecca Vitale, and Maia Cheslow. Thank you all for your hard work, and for what we know is an awful lot of dish washing.

Kristy Mucci, Maddy Martin, Nozlee Samadzadeh, Brette Warshaw, Francesca Gilberti, Miranda Rake, Martine Trelaun, Christina DiLaura, Alaina Sullivan, and Victoria Spencer have been invaluable arms of our editorial team, tackling everything from last-minute blog posting to Shop curation to party planning and anything in between. Along the way, they and we have had an enormous amount of help from a group of tireless editors and interns, including Allie Chaden, Caroline Vernick, Helen Hollyman, Will Levitt, Rona Moser, Katie Essenfeld, Lily Taylor, Rachel Berkman, Hadley Assail, Meghan Gourley, Rose Kelly, Laura Wing, Anna Hezel, Gabriella Paiella, and Laura Loesch-Quintin. Our editorial and intern staffs handle everything we throw at them (and it really is everything) not simply without complaint, but with their whole selves, with absolute enthusiasm, and for that we are always so grateful.

Jennifer Steinhauer, a longtime friend of the site, continues to be an official part of the family with her weekly column "Jenny's in the Kitchen," where she tells the dirty truth about being a working mother and about cooking for her family, the joys and lack thereof. At the beginning of 2012, we welcomed the green-thumbed Amy Pennington as a columnist. Her urban gardening know-how has brought full circle the emphasis we've always placed on cooking in season and (we hope) encouraged more of our incredible home cooks to become home gardeners as well. *Food News Journal*'s Fran Brennan and Shelly Peppel bravely and wholeheartedly adventured into food news with us, and we loved every minute of working with them. Year after year, Charlotte Druckman, coconspirator in our annual Piglet Tournament of Cookbooks, rounds up the best cookbooks and judges for three weeks of heated debate, and she always wears the best dress to the party.

Peter Steinberg, Kfir Shay, Jon Stavis, Amanda Li, Alain Benzaken, Camillia BenBasset, Gareth Geraty, and Oka Tai-Lee are the development and design magicians behind our site. With a click of the mouse or a tap-tap on the keyboard, they bring everything that we dream up into being, and it goes almost without saying that without them, we simply would not exist. We get additional digital help from our talented videographers Elena Parker and Drew Lavyne, who tastefully edit our onscreen antics and handle the often-haphazard nature of a Food52 video shoot with nothing but good humor.

We can't believe that it was over three years ago that we sat down to lunch at Aquavit with Bob Miller. Three sentences into an explanation of our vision for what Food52 would become, he was signing us up for these two cookbooks. We are grateful for his faith in us. Along the way, we've had a ball working with Cassie Jones, who has dealt so calmly with any and all of our various book-related fire drills, of which there have been many. Also at William Morrow, we're grateful to Jessica McGrady, Leah Carlson-Stanisic, Karen Lumley, Joyce Wong, Shelby Meizlik, Liate Stehlik, Lynn Grady, Tavia Kowalchuk, and Shawn Nichols.

Thanks also to Heather Schroder, Nicole Tourtelot, and Tabitha Schick at ICM; to Debbie Stier, the social media master who set us on the right path; and to our friends Gretchen Holt and Bena Shah at OXO, who have sponsored our contests from the very beginning and whose wares have made all of our winners very happy!

It takes a lot of work to keep Food52 in motion, and we are fortunate to receive an enormous amount of support from our family and friends. We would especially like to thank Jennifer Steinhauer; Eliza and Mike Anderson; Veronica Stubbs; Rhonda Thompson; our beloved children, Walker, Addie, and Clara; and, particularly, our sweet husbands, Jonathan Dorman and Tad Friend.

Amanda & Merrill

INDEX